THE TAO OF COACHING

THE TAO OF

KNOWLEDGEXCHANGE
Santa Monica

COACHING

Boost Your Effectiveness at Work
by Inspiring Those Around You

MAX LANDSBERG

Knowledge Exchange, LLC
1299 Ocean Avenue
Santa Monica, California 90401

Copyright © McKinsey & Company Inc. 1997
Cartoons copyright © HIGGINS 1997

Knowledge Exchange and the pyramid logo
are trademarks of Knowledge Exchange, LLC.

Quotes throughout this book are from *The Tao Te Ching of Lao Tzu,*
translated by Brian Browne Walker. Reprinted by permission of St. Martin's
Press Incorporated. Copyright ©1995 by Brian Walker.

Library of Congress Cataloging-in-Publication Data

Landsberg, Max
    The tao of coaching : boost your effectiveness at work by
    inspiring those around you / Max Landsberg
         p.   cm.
    Includes bibliograohical references and index.
    ISBN 1-888232-34-X (alk. paper)
    1. Employee motivation.   I. Title
HF5549.5.M63L364   1997
658.3'14--dc21   97-19284
                                CIP

Text design by Luci Goodman

1 2 3 4 5 6 7 8 9-VA-99 98 97
First printing March 1997
ISBN: 1-888232-34-x

To my parents, who remain
excellent coaches

CONTENTS

Introduction

Alex's Story

Increase your
effectiveness
as a leader

Help others
to develop
and grow

*The familiar yin-yang icon symbolizes
the harmonious interplay between apparent opposites.*

TYPICAL BELIEFS OF GREAT COACHES

You can't be a leader without a
following.

The autocratic boss is facing
extinction.

Investing ten minutes in coaching
will save an hour.

How to win friends and influence
people—become a great coach.

INTRODUCTION

COACHING: A VITAL SKILL FOR LEADERS

Would you like to:

Create more time for yourself?

Develop a band of colleagues who relish working with you?

Benefit from greater effectiveness, both among those who work for you and in your organization more broadly?

Build stronger skills in coaching, which you can apply both at work and beyond?

If so, you are not alone. You are one of a new breed of leaders who recognize that autocracy no longer works, yet empowerment alone is not enough. This new breed aspires to influence people and events by adopting the age-old skills of coaching. These skills were known to great masters and their apprentices of old, were lost in the dark ages of society's industrialization, but have lately been rediscovered by more effective organizations and teams.

The complexity inherent in today's business environment means that the autocrat is no longer in a position to make better decisions than subordinates are able to make collectively, can no longer be sufficiently omniscient to monitor everything, nor omnipresent enough to take all corrective actions needed. Yet, at the opposite extreme, the effectiveness of the purely "empowering" manager has not been proven.

So the new breed of manager employs a broader repertoire of management styles sometimes hands-on, sometimes hands-off, as suits the occasion. But she/he also makes extensive use of the coaching techniques illustrated in this book.

More practically, this new breed recognizes that even the master cannot do the whole job unaided; that the master-leader therefore has to delegate appropriately; that a following of able apprentices is a must for the truly effective leader; and that it is often the leader her/himself, rather than the training department, who is best placed to build the abilities of colleagues on the job.

The creed of the new-style leader includes the beliefs that investing ten minutes in coaching an apprentice will eventually save the master an hour; and that the twin notions of (1) helping others to develop and grow, and (2) increasing your effectiveness as a leader are simply two sides of the same coin.

That is why this book is called *The Tao of Coaching*. The practical philosophy of Taoism was first codified in China over 2,000 years ago and has three main elements, all of which are relevant to becoming a coach:

To bring about change or transformation, we must follow a "way" (or Tao).

The "way" involves a harmonious interplay between apparent opposites—for example, coach and coachee, asking and telling, developing the coachee's skills and delegating by the coach.

The "way" relies on as much on intuitive wisdom as it does on rational thought.

As you read this book—which aims to guide you toward becoming a better coach—I hope you will recognize the importance of these underlying themes.

So, what do we mean by coaching? Coaching aims to enhance the performance and learning ability of others. It involves providing feedback, but it also uses other techniques such as motivation, effective questioning, and consciously matching your management style to the coachee's readiness to undertake a particular task. It is based on helping the coachee to help her/himself through dynamic interaction—it does not rely on a one-way flow of telling and instructing.

A glance at the contents page of this book will show you the basic tool kit of the great coach. After reading the story in the following chapters, which is based on real-life experiences, you should be able to practice applying it.

The good news is that becoming an effective coach requires only that you develop some simple habits and build one or two basic interpersonal skills. With the inclination, and some practice, most people can become truly memorable coaches.

The best way to pick up these habits and skills, of course, is to work with one or more people who are already great coaches. You will see them in action, and see at first hand the benefits—both to themselves and to others—of what they do. These habits would sound simple in a lecture, but their true power only becomes apparent in a real-life setting.

As the next best thing to supplying such a real-life role model, this book aims to be a "pocket coach" by providing a linked set of parables drawn from the work life of a fictional person. It follows his career as he coaches, and is coached, both well and badly. Each chapter ends with a summary of the key lessons and suggestions on how to practice the illustrated habits and skills. To use this book effectively, you might want to:

1   *Skim through the story, identifying the situations or ideas which are most relevant to you now.*

2   *Complete a quick self-appraisal (Appendix 1, page 130). It will only take you a minute to complete and will provide real signposts to topics on which you could usefully work. Also ask people with whom you work to complete a copy of this form based on their impressions of you.*

3   *Pick a topic to practice this week—perhaps it's feedback, perhaps it's asking questions instead of telling. Practice other topics when they appear most relevant and valuable to you.*

4   *Reappraise yourself after a month, or ensure you elicit some "upward feedback" (see Chapter 3—Eliciting Feedback).*

In today's business environment, the successful manager needs to be as adept at "soft" skills, like coaching, as she/he is at "hard" skills, like finance and strategy. As Lee Iaccoca said, "Inventories can be managed, but people need to be led."

Of course there are situations in which coaching is inappropriate, where decisive or emergency action is called for. Consequently, this guide is intended to help you identify both where—and how—you can use coaching techniques for the direct benefits of yourself and others.

Max Landsberg
New York
January 1997

The great general doesn't show off his power.
A strong warrior doesn't get angry.

This is called the power of noncontention.
This is called using the strength of others.

THE MANAGER'S SKILLS IN COACHING ARE NOW REQUIRED AND REWARDED.

Flatter and more fluid organizational structures mean that bosses can no longer micromanage.

People—a company's most important asset—are increasingly attracted to organizations that will help them to develop.

Accelerating changes in business favor constant on-the-job training.

1 PROMOTION OR NOT?

Alex wondered whether this was his last chance. Although he had been promoted into a senior management position, it had taken a year longer than he had expected. The question now was whether he would be promoted to a Director position—and what would happen to him if he failed. It was now or never, and it wouldn't be plain sailing. "At least," he thought, "I've given it my best shot. I might as well enjoy my vacation."

Alex settled back into his chair beside the pool and gazed out over the Aegean, oblivious to the playful shrieks from the beach below. He tried to relax, but wished he'd arranged the vacation for two weeks later, after the Board back in London had made its decision.

He congratulated himself, however, on having rented a villa with one of the few telephones on the island which actually worked. Perhaps he'd get a call after the Board meeting? He glanced nervously over his shoulder to check that no one had accidentally left the phone off the hook, unplugged it, or otherwise reduced it to the normal state of telephones on the island.

As if by telepathy, the phone rang. Was it for Alex? It was! Was it his secretary Julia back at the office? It was! Was he now a Director? "I'm afraid they've had to delay the meeting until tomorrow—I thought I should let you know," she apologized.

"No problem," he said, cursing inaudibly. "I'll speak to you again soon."

He realized that he was in danger of not really having a vacation at all...if only he could see into the future...or consult an oracle.

He thought about last week's day trip to Delphi. What were the words carved above the gateway to the Oracle's chair, to prepare the ancient inquirers on their way to the prophet? That's it: Know thyself!

"OK," he resolved, "half an hour of introspection, my own decision on whether I deserve to be a Director, and then unadulterated vacation."

The problem was in some sense straightforward. Alex knew that, on the plus side, he had led a major reorganization, implemented a courageous acquisition, and turned around an unprofitable subsidiary. The only minus—but it had been a major one—was that he had on occasion tended to use people and burnt them out. He had acquired a reputation as a "people-eater"; at one point it had reached a stage where no one really wanted to work for him, or with him.

Five years earlier, the Board might have overlooked this character flaw. But now the management skills and habits necessary for building people's abilities, for helping them to develop, for coaching them, had assumed far greater importance. A deficiency in this area would not go unnoticed.

Deep down, Alex knew that this new emphasis on people development had been driven by several powerful forces which were now affecting most large companies. First had been a trend towards reducing the number of management levels in organizations' hierarchies—that is, delayering. Everyone was now working in cross-functional teams for large proportions of their time. No longer were jobs and roles prescribed and static, so no longer could bosses just go on telling subordinates exactly what to do. Rather, the successful companies were now those in which people learned new skills and habits from each other, and in which managers were also coaches.

Second, labor markets had changed. The most able people now knew that companies with a coaching culture did exist, and that it was much more fun and rewarding to work there. In addition, people were more mobile, and excellent organizations were focusing more on bringing out their people's potential to retain their best performers.

Third, business conditions, markets and technologies were now changing even more rapidly than in the past. This meant that companies could no longer rely on providing employees with a week or two of off-site training courses every year. Training now had to be continuous and on the job—by coaching.

"Well," mused Alex, "am I good enough at this coaching stuff?" Intuitively he thought he was indeed now a good coach. He hadn't been a natural at it when he joined the company a few years ago, but he'd picked up a few good coaching habits along the way. These had helped him to become much more effective as a manager, so he kept an eye open for more tips from coaches who were role models. He had also read a great book on the subject, and had put into practice many of its suggestions. His only problem had come about a year ago when pressures to achieve caused him to slip back into some bad old habits, resulting in his failure to be promoted.

But he had decided to mend his ways, and people now wanted to work with him again. He even found that his personal relationships outside work had improved.

In terms of coaching, Tao means "the way in which I work and live in order to derive energy from interacting dynamically with people and things as opposed to expending energy by continually going against the grain." Yin is building the skills and abilities of those who work with us, and yang is becoming more effective by delegating to those people whom we have helped to become more able.

On balance, he was about to promote himself to Director. To be absolutely certain of his decision, however, he decided to review his own moments of truth in coaching during his time with the company. This would allow him to reach a well-informed decision. It would also provide the basis for lending his weight to the company-wide coaching program—his avowed mission if he was indeed promoted to the Board.

With the benefit of hindsight, Alex began to review how much he'd learned about coaching—not only from his own coaching practices as a senior manager but also from his early experiences of having been coached by others.

He picked up his hand-held dictating machine and began to speak, recalling the lessons of his career since he'd first joined the company.

This is Alex's story...

People who know aren't full of facts.
People who are full of facts don't know.

STAR MANAGERS USE MANY DIFFERENT TYPES OF INTERACTION, RANGING FROM "ASKING" TO "TELLING."

Practice using effective questions
(even when you know the answer),
as one of the most powerful
coaching tools.

Be clear about **why** you are using a
particular type of interaction.

Merely "telling" is rarely the best
way to build someone's skills.

2 ASKING VERSUS TELLING

Alex was tearing his hair out. He had just joined the company as a manager of strategic planning, and was halfway through his first project. He was used to gathering facts on market trends and analyzing lots of numbers, but he wasn't used to writing the succinct reports that seemed to be the norm in his new company. He had developed what he thought was a creative title page for his document: "Acquisition in the ice-cream market—cold logic or soft option?" But he was having real problems in structuring his thoughts for the main body of the report.

He took a deep breath and set off down the corridor to find Bob, his boss.

"You need to start with the main message," Bob explained, "and then structure the supporting rationale—ideally into three points, because most audiences can easily assimilate three points—in one of two ways. Either use a grouping of parallel points or use a logical flow of argument: statement, implication, resolution. I have to go to a meeting now, but let's meet up later to run through your draft." Alex had been confused by this rapid set of instructions, which hadn't made immediate sense to him, and by the end of the afternoon had not made much progress.

Alex wondered whether Sarah could help. As a senior marketing manager, she had been involved in recruiting Alex into the company, and he suspected that she had been influential in the decision to offer him the job. She and Alex had many things in common—they had both been to the same business school, they were both interested in direct marketing, and they were both accomplished tennis players.

Sarah was sympathetic to Alex's plight in structuring the report. "What's the most extreme statement you would feel comfortable making about this ice-cream market?" she asked.

"Well, I'm not yet sure that we should actually enter the market, but it does look attractive," he replied.

"And why does it look attractive?"

"Well, demand is rising, profit margins look sustainable, competition does not seem to be very intense, and prices have held up over the last five years."

"I see," she replied, "and are any of these four points really different sides of the same coin?"

"I guess the point about pricing is really part of the statement about profit margins. Hey," he continued excitedly, "I think I've got something on costs, too. So, I could say that the market is attractive because: (1) demand is rising; (2) profit margins are sustainable on both the price and cost side; and (3) competitors look likely to remain weak."

"Thanks, Sarah. I think I can work on this structure. By the way, is this a grouping of reasons or a flow of argument? It looks like a grouping of reasons to me...."

Alex was impressed by Sarah's approach. By spending just four minutes with him, instead of Bob's two minutes, she had really helped him with structuring the report—and she didn't even know anything about the ice-cream market! She had just asked the right questions. He also felt more confident about drafting the next report, and thought he'd probably be able to learn a lot from working with Sarah in the future, if the opportunity arose.

Sarah, too, thought that the brief interaction had been worthwhile; she believed that Alex had a lot of raw talent, and hoped to coopt him to work on one of her projects in the future.

"Ludwig, are you deaf or what? If I've told you once, I've told you a thousand times, drop the music schoozic and get a proper job..."

THE COACHING SPECTRUM

Socrates saw himself as a "midwife to understanding." He believed that one could **help** people understand, but that one could not **make** people understand—just as a midwife delivers, but does not give birth to, the child.

Similarly, the coach is a midwife to skill building, not typically a highly didactic teacher. And the coach's most important decision is whether to issue an instruction or to ask a question—or to use a style of interaction somewhere between these two extremes. You will face this decision in a wide variety of coaching situations—when deciding the topic on which to help the coachee, when providing feedback or when helping the coachee decide what to do next.

At work, many bosses rely on **telling** others—directly or indirectly—what to do and (sometimes) how to do it. But as a coach, it's important to have a broader range of approaches in your repertoire. Often, the **pivotal question** is more powerful than the instruction, as Socrates knew.

If there is one thing you do differently as a result of reading this book, it should be simply to try **asking** a few good questions where you might otherwise have issued an instruction or leapt into providing advice, as illustrated by Alex's story on the preceding pages.

E X E R C I S E
Review Appendix 2, page 132.

THE ASK/TELL SPECTRUM

← More Empowering			More Controlling →	
Ask Questions and Paraphrase	**Make Suggestions**	**Demonstrate**	**Give Advice**	**Tell What and How**

Benefit

Higher, if coachee has reasonable skills and at least one creative idea to bring	**Quality of Task Completion**	Lower, unless the coachee's role is to repeat a relatively simple task that has little scope for being redesigned
Deeper understanding	**Learning by Coaching**	Deep understanding, but only if the coach is a true expert
Higher in most cases	**Motivation by Coachee**	Lower, unless coachee feels completely lost
Slightly more, depending on speed of coachee's learning	**Intial Time from Coachee**	Slightly less, assuming that the task can be specified easily, and that the coachee understands, and follows the instructions
Potentially higher	**Learning by Coaching**	Very little
Tasks which the coachee will probably need to repeat in some form	**When to Use**	"Mission-critical" tasks where failure would lead to disaster; very simple tasks

In the pursuit of learning, everyday something is added.
See the subtle—and be illuminated.

OBTAINING FEEDBACK FROM OTHERS CAN BOOST YOUR OWN SKILLS AND DEVELOPMENT.

Choose the right person to ask.

Make it easy for them to give feedback.

3 ELICITING FEEDBACK

Six months into his career with the company, Alex was feeling satisfied with his progress. He thought he understood how the company operated, and he had already made some substantial contributions. Although he didn't yet manage anyone else, he had practiced his "effective questioning" technique to good effect. On more than one occasion, he had constructively changed the course of a meeting through a well-planted question—even though he already knew the answer.

But one thing still puzzled him. "How on earth do I find out how well I'm doing? No one ever seems to tell me directly."

The ice-cream project had been moved to the back burner—a move which Alex thought had obvious dangers! And Alex was now working with Bob, his boss, on a project to streamline the company's production processes. He had been looking forward to the project, since he thought he had some particularly relevant skills to contribute. After all, he had studied engineering at his university and had then worked as a production manager for two years before going to business school.

The project had started well. Alex had developed a good working relationship with Bob and felt that his work so far had been of real value. He had even had his first opportunity to make a full presentation to the divisional board. However, he realized that he was not getting much coaching or feedback. He had broached the subject tentatively with Bob a few times, including immediately after the last presentation. But Bob had merely responded that Alex seemed to be doing very well—and was, in fact, exceeding Bob's expectations.

Alex decided to seek Sarah's advice, and took the opportunity to sit next to her at lunch in the cafeteria.

"Sarah, I can't seem to get Bob to tell me how I'm performing. How do *you* manage to elicit helpful and constructive feedback?"

Her response was disarmingly simple. "You have to ask, and you have to listen."

Several days later, Alex tried it out. "Bob, could we have half an hour together, so that you could give me some feedback on how I've been doing for the last couple of months?"

"OK, Alex, but what would you like feedback on? I'm a bit surprised that you're asking for feedback, because I didn't really think that you wanted any."

It's up to you to obtain feedback from others.

"What made you think that?" quizzed an astonished Alex.

"Well, you didn't take the initiative to talk through with me, when we started the project, the areas in which you wanted to build your skills. Also, the one time I did try to give you some feedback, you seemed very defensive."

Alex did not want to become confrontational, but he did point out his two subsequent attempts to discuss his performance.

"Yes, I remember," Bob replied, "but both requests were in front of several other people. I got the impression that you were merely seeking public acclaim. That said, I'm sorry for not following up later on. Anyway, on what specific area would you like to have my feedback?"

Alex was unsure. He had assumed that Bob, with his greater experience, would know exactly what to focus on. However, they agreed to meet the next day, after Alex had thought about the areas in which he would most value some help.

> **Coachees can often learn more if the coach asks them how well they've performed a particular task than from being told, "Here's what you did wrong, and here's what to do next time."**

They focused on Alex's strengths and weaknesses in delivering presentations, and had a highly productive half hour. Bob helped Alex to realize that he needed to establish eye contact with each person in the audience instead of with only one person, and that he needed to set the context more clearly at the beginning of his presentation.

As Alex left Bob's office he really did feel coached—rather than evaluated; Bob had been careful to discuss specific examples of what Alex had done, rather than talking about character traits. Alex also had a clear plan of action.

"I suppose that obtaining feedback is as easy as ask and listen," thought Alex, "although both you and your coach need to know enough about you to address the right topics, and you have to be careful to listen with an open mind, and without being defensive."

Alex had jotted down the points on the following two pages for future reference, and had found them as helpful later on—when he had become a more senior manager—as they had been on that day. He also recalled a fragment of a poem which he had learned by heart as a schoolboy:

If you can trust yourself when all men doubt you,
But make allowance for their doubting too...

RUDYARD KIPLING

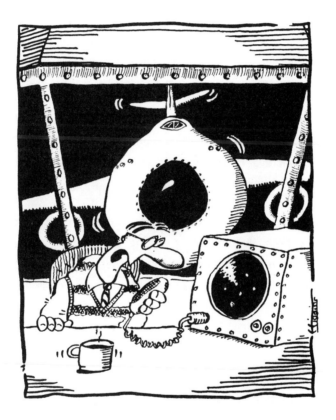

"Oh, is that so. Well I'm the Top Banana,
Head Honcho, Big Cheese, around here,
and I say you're at thirty thousand feet!"

GETTING FEEDBACK

When was the last time that you received useful feedback? Probably too long ago: few people ever feel that they receive enough feedback. This is true for older as well as for younger people. For the experienced as well as for the inexperienced. For the able as well as for the less able.

Although the primary focus of this book is on how to be a great coach, it is worth touching on the skill of being a great coachee. It's a valuable skill for the workplace, as well as for life in general. Managers who fail to receive feedback (for whatever reason) disable an important self-correcting mechanism and aid to personal productivity.

However, you cannot be a furtive coachee—you have to make it clear that you want feedback. In addition, in asking for feedback you are asking someone to do you a favor (one that requires some courage on the coach's part), so you should also make the process as easy as possible for her/him. The facing page provides some suggestions.

EXERCISE

Identify two people from whom you would value feedback this week, and ask for it. See Appendix 3, page 135.

GETTING FEEDBACK:
MAKING IT EASY FOR THE GIVER

1 Choose the right coach for the right topic—a coach whom you really trust. For example, you might want to choose different peers/subordinates/bosses/friends, depending on whether you feel you need feedback on:

- Management style (choose someone whom you manage).
- Presentation skills (alert a member of your audience).

2 Give your coach as much notice as possible, so that she/he can marshal relevant examples.

- Explain at the beginning of major pieces of work what you would like—for example, feedback topics and the frequency of discussion.
- Remind your coach prior to the meeting—don't just show up.

3 Take the initiative in building a trusting relationship.

- Volunteer your own perspective on areas in which you could improve (don't just try to highlight areas in which you are phenomenally excellent)
- Explain what motivates you and what demotivates you; disclose other factors that might be relevant.

4 Receive the feedback genuinely.

- Avoid being defensive (unless you never want feedback again!)
- Follow what the coach says—show your genuine interest, summarize what you are learning, and ask for specific examples and explanations.

5 Show your appreciation.

- Make real progress, and follow at least some of the advice.
- Let the coach know that she/he has made a difference; thank the coach.

The wise person...creates without possessing,
nourishes without demanding.

COACHING IS A NORMAL PART OF GOOD MANAGEMENT—NOT EXTRA WORK. EXPECT TO REAP THE REWARDS.

Recognize that coaching is more than just giving great feedback.

Expect many benefits to you— the coach. It's not just the coachee who gains.

Expect a rapid payback on your investment in coaching time.

4 CORRECTING COMMON COACHING MYTHS

It had been three weeks since Alex had seen Sarah in the cafeteria, and he decided to drop by her office. "Hi, Alex, I haven't seen you for a while, how are you?"

"Fine, thanks," he replied. "By the way, thanks for your advice on obtaining feedback. I had a really useful session with Bob."

"That's great," said Sarah, "and I'm glad you dropped by, because I was wondering if *you* could do *me* a favor. As you may know, the company's Human Resources Committee is taking a real interest in coaching. As part of the overall project, I thought we should have an article on the topic in the company magazine. Perhaps a few key hints on how to do it, plus a section on why to do it. I've drafted a few pages, and I was hoping you'd be willing to review them and let me have your reaction."

"I'd be happy to," he replied, with a slightly confused expression. "But isn't it fairly straightforward? I mean, don't people just provide feedback and coaching to help other people get better at their work?"

For the first time, Sarah looked at him condescendingly. "Well, Alex, there's slightly more to it than that. In fact, the great coach has as many selfish reasons as philanthropic ones to invest a few minutes a day in deploying his or her skills in this area. Anyway, if you have a moment to read through my draft, I'd be very grateful."

"*The Myths of Coaching*—seems like a good title," he mumbled, as he left Sarah's office with the draft document.

THE MYTHS OF COACHING

by Sarah Jennings

There are five major myths surrounding what it takes to be a good coach. Here's an attempt to set the record straight.

Let's face it, coaching is not about being a nice guy. It's about bringing the same structure and creativity to your interactions with colleagues as you bring to solving business problems. But before we go any further in defining what it takes to be a good coach, let's address head-on some of coaching's myths and realities.

MYTH

We coach primarily to help others.

REALITY

There are many tangible, selfish and acceptable reasons for one to become a great coach. In fact, good coaches find the personal payoffs so high that they rarely kick the habit. The following—listed in order of decreasing selfishness—is a sample of those payoffs:

> More time for yourself. You can either go home earlier or invest the time in higher quality work. While it's virtually impossible to prove, most great coaches believe that investing just ten minutes a day in coaching teammates typically generates at least 20 minutes of extra time per day for the coach.

Better customer relations skills. By coaching colleagues you can hone the interpersonal skills which you need for building effective relations with customers and clients.

Stronger organization. If you plan on a long-term career with the company, investing in the development of your colleagues is clearly worthwhile.

More fun. You and others working in coaching-oriented teams tend to enjoy yourselves more.

Stronger following. If you help others, they tend to help you. And if you aspire to be a leader, it's worth remembering that every leader needs a following.

MYTH

Focus on the coachee.

REALITY

Know thyself. Coaches don't focus exclusively on the coachee. In fact, great coaches have a high degree of self-awareness. We all have the basic skills to coach; unfortunately, most of us have a few psychological blocks when it comes to applying those skills well and consistently. Great coaches know how to overcome their own blocks.

MYTH

Coaching equals feedback.

REALITY

There are many other important coaching tools and habits. While most people think that coaching is merely providing feedback and suggestion to coachees, the truth is that insightful feedback is only one tool in the coach's tool box. For example, good coaches typically master the art of effective questioning. Coachees can often learn more from a coach asking,

"How well do you think you did; what might you do differently next time?" than from being told, "Here's what you did wrong, and here's what to do next time." There are also other tools, like the GROW approach and motivation techniques.

MYTH

Coaching requires a lot of time.

REALITY

The best coaching comes in small doses. Many people believe that coaching comes in large quantums. But with a bit of practice, you don't need to change into a jogging suit every time you want to provide coaching. Small investments of time—as little as five minutes—can yield tangible increases in performance.

MYTH

Coaching is about work.

REALITY

Good coaching will spread to other areas of life. Those who develop their coaching skills at work usually find they are better able to help their friends, partners and children. In that respect, coaching is clearly a **life skill.**

"So just to re-cap, I like to be rubbed here, stroked there and massaged here, but don't ever fidget with this bit..."

Therefore the sage does what is right
without acting righteous,
points without piercing, straightens without straining,
and enlightens without dazzling.

AID WILL HELP YOU DELIVER FEEDBACK WELL.

Action that the coachee took.

Impact (positive or negative) that
the actions had.

Desired outcome (if the coachee
were to do the same task
differently).

5 Giving Feedback

Two weeks later, as Alex was reading Sarah's article on the myths of coaching in the company magazine, he thought about Gordon. Perhaps it was worth investing some time in coaching him.

Gordon, who had just graduated from the university and had recently joined the company, was the first person who Alex had had reporting directly to him. The company had renewed its interest in the ice-cream market and Alex, with Gordon's help, had been asked to advise on whether to acquire a large manufacturer of ice cream and frozen yogurt—Cones-and-Tubs International.

Things had started well: they had assembled the relevant facts, interviewed some of the company's customers, and estimated how much Cones-and-Tubs was worth.

Alex, however, had noticed that Gordon tended to disappear for long periods of time. He was undoubtedly working very hard, because whenever Alex managed to catch up with him, he always had reams of printout from his personal computer, with all sorts of weird and wonderful scenarios analyzed in minute detail.

The problem was that Gordon had clearly gone off on a tangent on many occasions, and Alex felt sure this was because he had not really been paying attention in the team meetings which they had held periodically.

"Time for some feedback," thought Alex, as he flicked through a booklet on giving constructive feedback which Sarah had given him.

The section on delivering feedback started with the usual caveats that there was more to coaching than just giving feedback; that feedback was, however, a critically important tool; and that it was difficult to generalize about how to do it well. Nevertheless, it continued, in providing feedback, you should ensure that you address three topics, with the acronym AID to help you remember them:

A

ACTION

The things that the coachee is doing well, or poorly, in the area under review.

I

IMPACT

The effect these actions are having.

D

DESIRED OUTCOME

The positive impact the coachee would have by doing things differently.

Alex had just closed the booklet when Gordon dropped by for the prearranged meeting. Alex started by reviewing the project's good progress to date, and congratulated Gordon on several aspects of his work so far. Then he continued, "Gordon, I'd like to give you some feedback on your participation in our team meetings. Would you find that helpful?" Gordon nodded his assent.

"Well, I couldn't help noticing that you sometimes don't appear fully engaged in our team discussions. For example, at the meeting yesterday you seemed to be doodling, and even staring out of the window on occasion. Would you say that was an accurate observation?" (*Description of actions.*)

"I do sometimes feel a bit bored by the endless discussions," Gordon replied. "I suppose I'd just prefer to be getting on with the analysis."

"OK, Gordon, but the problem this causes is that when the meeting has finished, and you go off to do your part of the work, you don't take account of changes in direction which everyone else has agreed to at the meeting. As a result, some of your work ends up being redundant, and you come across as rather arrogant, since it appears that you can't be bothered to listen to what your teammates are saying." (*Description of impact.*)

> **Guide—don't judge—when coaching.**

"I recognize the first point about redundant work, but I didn't realize that I would seem arrogant," replied Gordon, surprised.

"Let's see what we can do to address the situation," suggested Alex. "Do you have any ideas for getting more engaged in these meetings?" (*Discussion of desired outcome.*)

Gordon didn't have any immediate ideas; it was, after all, his first real job and he wasn't used to working in teams. So Alex continued, "How about if we arrange for you to present your most recent work at the beginning of each meeting? Or, better still, why don't we expand your role on the project to include helping me in the overall coordination? That way you would have a reason to keep track of what's going on. Perhaps you could even summarize the agreed next steps at the end of each meeting, before everyone leaves the room."

Over the next few weeks Gordon became much more engaged in proceedings, his teammates stopped moaning about him, and Alex found that he could delegate many of the project coordination tasks to Gordon. Alex felt that the AID structure was both simple and effective; he'd try to use it more often in the future.

**Annual appraisals with Old "Sparky" Watson
tended to be a little traumatic...**

PROVIDING FEEDBACK

Providing feedback is one of the coach's most important skills. Narrowly defined, it means replaying to the coachee what she/he did in a specific situation. More broadly—and more usefully—defined, it includes highlighting the impact of what the coachee did. It also includes a discussion of what the coachee might do (even) better next time.

A few definitions:

Positive feedback applies to situations where the coachee did a good job. It consists of simple praise, but is even more powerfully reinforcing when the coach specifically highlights why or how the coachee did a good job.

Constructive feedback highlights how the coachee could do better next time. It needs to be delivered sensitively.

• Use the AID mnemonic suggested earlier.

• When describing the coachee's actions, focus on specific observable facts ("In the last presentation you did not fully address some of the follow-up questions."), not assumed traits ("You tend to be evasive.").

Negative feedback—that is, merely replaying something that went wrong—is essentially destructive and is only used, usually by accident, to terminate friendships and marriages. It describes a perceived negative behavior, without proposing a resolution ("You're always complaining.").

PROVIDING FEEDBACK

Bad Feedback	Good Feedback	Hallmarks of Good Feedback
Creates defensiveness and confrontation; focuses on blame	Creates trust and cooperation; focuses on improvements—possible or achieved	• Create a contract to discuss issues • Acknowledge coachee's feelings
Does not improve skill	Increases skill	• Focus on **skills** not **person** • Paint specific picture of desired skill • Suggest practical steps
Undermines confidence and self-esteem	Improves confidence in ability and potential	• Position as need to **build** or **demonstrate** vs. "don't have" or "must prove" • Balance negatives and positives; provide constructive actions
Leaves person guessing	Clarifies "exactly where I stand" and "what to do next"	• Verify with questions; ask for coachee's recap • Jointly arrive at plan
Leaves person feeling **judged**	Leaves person feeling **helped**	• Invite coachee to assess own performance first • Offer support for future

EXERCISE

Identify someone to whom you could provide useful feedback today (see Appendix 4, page 137), and follow through.

A good runner leaves no tracks; a good speaker makes no slips;
a good planner doesn't have to scheme.

FOR GREATER IMPACT IN LESS TIME, GIVE

A CLEAR STRUCTURE TO COACHING

SESSIONS BY USING **GROW:**

GOALS

REALITY

OPTIONS

WRAP-UP

6

STRUCTURING THE COACHING SESSION

Alex jumped at the knock on his office door. "How are you, Alex? I hear that you are developing a reputation for providing useful feedback."

It was Michael, the Chief Financial Officer of the company. Although he was senior to Alex, he was a part-time member of the multi-functional team—Project Quest—which Alex was leading to advise on the acquisition of Cones-and-Tubs International.

It was only 3 p.m., but Alex looked drained. "I'm fine, thanks," he replied without conviction.

"Alex, why not put the work down for half an hour? I can see that something is causing you a problem. Perhaps I can help."

Alex accepted the offer gratefully. He had a particularly open relationship with Michael, who had been his informal mentor ever since their doubles victory in the company's annual tennis championship. "I've been with the company for just over a year now, and find that I'm spending a lot of time running meetings. But I can't seem to get the discussions to make as much progress as I'd like. Perhaps I'm doing something wrong."

"I can spare you 20 minutes," Michael offered, "why don't we see if we can figure out something to help you. But first, what is your **goal**—both regarding the management of meetings in general, and for our next

20 minutes together in particular? In other words, if I could grant you one wish for this session, what would it be?"

"I suppose it would be to have a brief checklist for how to manage meetings better."

"And do you think we can accomplish that in the next 20 minutes?" Michael inquired.

"Let's give it a go, Michael, there's nothing to lose—I feel a lot better already, even thinking that there might be a solution."

Michael asked Alex to be more specific about the **reality** of the situation. Just how did Alex know that there really was a problem? Were there particular situations in which he felt more, or less, able to manage the dynamics of meetings? What solutions had he tried so far? Of course, Michael had himself been a participant in many of the meetings which Alex had been chairing, and so was able to offer one or two of his own observations. However, he knew that it was Alex who had to do the diagnosis if the ideas were to be useful.

Initially, Alex had felt that the main reason for his difficulty was a lack of ability in dealing with several awkward team members. But with Michael's guidance in thinking things through, he also realized that he didn't pay enough attention to planning the meetings in advance. "So, Alex, which topic would you like to focus on—people or planning?"

"Let's talk about planning the meetings," replied Alex. "I'll need to put in some more thought before addressing the issue of how to interact with difficult team members."

"OK, so let's focus on the **options** you have. What could you try? What have you seen work well in similar circumstances? Try to be radical."

Alex reflected for a moment. "I suppose I could put more thought into my preparations for the meeting."

"How do you mean?" probed Michael, moving to the flipchart.

"Well, currently I prepare an agenda with a simple list of the topics for discussion. In future I could be more focused and actually list the specific issues we need to resolve. I could even list the team's hypotheses for resolving each issue—and circulate it prior to the meeting. That way we could really be focused." Alex was beginning to look relieved, and he continued to brainstorm other ideas for better meeting preparation, with Michael throwing in occasional ideas of his own. (Michael even made a mental note of some of these ideas for his own subsequent use.)

"Time to **wrap up**," said Michael, glancing at his watch. "Do you think you'll actually do any of this? What are the next steps? What support do you need, if any?"

> Use the four-step structure GROW to move effectively through a coaching session.
>
> Use both "ask" and "tell" within each step of the process.
>
> Iterate flexibly between the four steps.

Alex was sure that he would adopt the ideas they had just come up with—they would certainly be helpful. He also felt that he understood himself a little better, and would have more confidence to address similar issues in future. "The only further favor I would ask, Michael, is that you give me a kick under the table at the next meeting if I haven't done any of the preparation in advance!"

"Goal, Reality, Options, Wrap-up," thought Michael, as he was about to leave Alex's office. "That structure always seems to work if you want to have a really effective coaching session which goes beyond simply providing feedback."

"By the way, Alex, I really think we'll get approval for this ice-cream acquisition. I've even heard your name mentioned as the person to run the post-merger integration project—and that would probably mean a promotion. Of course, I'd be involved in the project too, as would Sarah Jennings on the marketing side. Do you know Sarah? I think you'd enjoy working with her."

As he entered the back straight, Dave faced
seven oncoming speedwalkers and the
dawning realization that he might have
started off in the wrong direction.

STRUCTURING A COACHING SESSION USING GROW

So, how do we actually structure a coaching session? The **GROW** (**G**oal, **Re**ality, **O**ptions, **W**rap-up) model is one of the most common coaching tools, widely used by many great coaches.

The framework provides a simple four-step structure for a coaching session. During the first step of a session (Goal), coach and coachee agree on a specific topic and objective for the discussion. During the second step (Reality), both coach and coachee invite self-assessment and offer specific examples to illustrate their points. They then move into the third step (Options), where suggestions are offered and choices made. And finally (Wrap-up), the coach and coachee commit to action, define a timeframe for their objectives and identify how to overcome possible obstacles.

Here are a few tips for using this model:

Use more **ask** than **tell**; elicit useful ideas from your coachee—don't just try to prove you are smart.

Think creatively—not just systematically—particularly in the Options and Wrap-up steps.

Illustrate and check understanding throughout by using specific examples—from the coachee's and your own experiences.

If you have a follow-up session, you can obviously lengthen or shorten each of the four steps as needed.

THE GROW MODEL

- Agree on topic for discussion
- Agree on specific objective of session
- Set long-term aim if appropriate

- Invite self-assessment
- Offer specific examples of feedback
- Avoid or check assumptions
- Discard irrelevant history

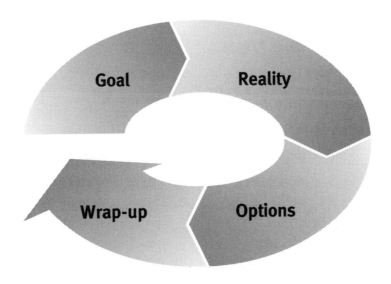

- Commit to action
- Identify possible obstacles
- Make steps specific and define timing
- Agree on support

- Cover the full range of options
- Invite suggestions from the coachee
- Offer suggestions carefully
- Ensure choices are made

EXERCISE

Find an opportunity to apply GROW this week.
See Appendix 5 (page 139) for examples of
questions to use.

Relinquish what is without.
Cultivate what is within.

DO **NOT** TREAT PEOPLE AS EQUALS.

Recognize their differences.

Coach each individual in a way that plays to their receptiveness.

Be explicit on how you will get differing types to work together.

7

DIAGNOSING
INDIVIDUALS'
DIFFERENT STYLES

A couple of weeks later, Alex was beginning to feel that his life was more under control, thanks to Michael's advice on the GROW framework. But he still had problems with Tom and Dick, the two members of the Project Quest team who were always arguing.

Alex was unsure whether to just knock their heads together or whether a more probing approach would have greater and more lasting value. At the end of a meeting with Michael, Alex sought his advice on Tom and Dick. Michael did not beat about the bush.

"I've met them both a few times, Alex. I'll bet you that Tom's an ENFP, and that Dick's an ISTJ." Alex looked completely blank, so Michael continued, "Do you know anything about psychology?" Alex shook his head, suddenly thinking that it was a bit absurd that managers were rarely taught much about what makes people tick.

"Well," continued Michael, "luckily, you don't need a degree in psychology to be an effective manager and coach, but you do need some way to figure out the different styles of interaction different people prefer to use."

"Personally, I recommend something called the Myers-Briggs Type Indicator. It sounds complex, but it's really quite simple. I'll give you a two-minute description, but then I suggest you read a booklet on the subject.

"The Type Indicator provides a description of how people prefer to operate in their daily lives. You know how, in meetings for example, some people like to stick rigidly to the agenda while others prefer to leap from idea to idea? The first type of person could well be an ISTJ, while the other might be an ENFP. If you know what type a person is, it will help you a good deal in interacting with them—and in helping them to work with each other.

"'So,' I hear you ask, 'what do these letters stand for?' The Indicator is based on four dimensions of how people prefer to operate. The first dimension relates to how they are *energized*—what turns them on. An Introvert (I) is energized by the inner world of thoughts and ideas, whereas an Extrovert (E) is energized by the outer world of people and things.

> **The Myers-Briggs Type Indicator was developed by the mother-daughter team of Katharine Briggs and Isabel Briggs Myers in the 1940s and is based on the theoretical work of Carl Jung. It is based on how a person prefers to respond to particular situations.**

"The second dimension describes what the person prefers to pay *attention* to. A Senser (S) focuses on facts and the five senses, while, at the other end of the spectrum, an Intuiter (N) type focuses on what might be, and the sixth sense.

"The third dimension describes how the person prefers to *make decisions*. The Thinker (T) tends to use reason and logic, while the Feeler (F) tends to use values and subjective judgement.

"The final dimension describes the person's *overall approach to life*—with Judgers (J) preferring to be planned and organized, while Perceivers

(P) prefer spontaneity and flexibility. If you take all the combinations, you'll find that these dimensions define 16 basic types of people."

Alex thought he understood. "So, an ISTJ person (who prefers to be an Introvert and Senser and Thinker and Judger) might think that an ENFP person (Extrovert, Intuiter, Feeler, Perceiver) was lax and disorganized, while the latter would think of the other as unimaginative and afraid of ever taking a leap into the dark? OK, I think I can see how I could use this, but how would I really know someone's type?"

> **Great teams overcome differences in individuals' preferred styles of working.**

"Sounds like an ISTJ kind of question, Alex! You can either have your team complete a standard questionnaire, if you think they're up to sharing the results. Otherwise, you'll just have to use your intuition. Why not have a chat with Tom and Dick separately, with these thoughts in mind, but don't forget to read the caveats in the booklet."

Alex set off down the corridor to find Tom. He had always thought that Tom's office was a disorganized mess, but now he understood a little better why this might not bother someone who valued flexibility, creativity, and spontaneity.

After his discussions with both Tom and Dick, Alex concluded that the original diagnosis had been correct; far from there being some deep-seated enmity between them, they just had very different preferred styles of working. He knew he had two options: either to reassign Tom and/or

Dick to parts of the project in which they would not have to work together, or to address the issue head-on. The latter approach had the advantages that (1) Tom and Dick would not have to get up to speed in new areas of work, and (2) the team could actually be more effective if these two team members could contribute their differing skills in a complementary way.

Alex opted for this latter course. In fact, he had everyone on the team, including himself, complete Type Indicator questionnaires, and share their results. Tom and Dick were wary of each other for a few days, but soon settled down to productive collaboration, based on their better understanding of each other. Not surprisingly, Tom focused on coming up with creative ideas, and Dick on checking their practicality.

However, Alex was surprised to discover that, by the time Project Quest was completed, Tom and Dick had shared their thoughts on what they had consciously learnt from each other. Tom had mapped out the things he could do to be more organized when the occasion required it, and Dick had done likewise for creativity. Alex decided to encourage this type of mutual learning more actively in the future.

Alex reflected on how valuable it was for team members, managers and coaches to have some simple model of how people interact, and to discuss this topic openly. He also realized how many misunderstandings derive from differences in style—rather than the most common interpretation: that the other party is dim-witted or has poor intentions.

"But what's really powerful," he thought, "is when you have real insights about individuals' styles, and combine them with the basic tools of coaching—asking effective questions, listening actively, providing clear feedback and using the GROW framework."

Thompson and Maguire may not have seen
eye to eye, but they were the best forensic
team on the Force...

UNDERSTANDING PREFERRED STYLES

There are many models for identifying and characterizing the styles of interaction which we and others prefer to employ. A widely used approach is the Myers-Briggs Type Indicator* (MBTI). It is based on the following four dimensions of a person's preferred approach to life.

1   How you are energized (Extrovert vs. Introvert).

2   What you pay attention to (Sensing vs. Intuition).

3   How you make decisions (Thinking vs. Feeling).

4   How you live and work (Judgement vs. Perception).

To work effectively with someone, take their preferred style into account. For example, Judgement types can become irritated by Perception types who may stray from the agenda. Conversely, people strong on Perception may see those who prefer Judgement as unwilling to take the time to explore creative options.

The characteristics of each dimension are indicated opposite. For a more complete description, see **Please Understand Me**, by David Keirsey and Marilyn Bates.

For more information about receiving a profile, contact:

Consulting Psychologists Press, Inc.,
3803 East Bayshore Road, Palo Alto, California 94303

*The description of the MBTI has been modified and reproduced by special permission of the publisher, Consulting Psychologists Press, Inc., Palo Alto, CA 94303 from **Introduction to Type,** by Isabel Briggs Myers. Copyright 1993 by Consulting Psychologists Press. All rights reserved. Further reproduction is prohibited without the publisher's written consent.

MYERS-BRIGGS TYPE INDICATOR: KEY ELEMENTS

1. Energizing (direction of energy)

Extrovert (E)	Introvert (I)
• External	• Internal
• Outside thrust	• Inside pull
• Blurt it out	• Keep it in
• Breadth	• Depth
• People, things	• Ideas, thoughts
• Interaction	• Concentration
• Action	• Reflection
• Do-think-do	• Think-to-do

2. Attending (perception)

Sensing (S)	Intutition (I)
• The 5 senses	• 6th sense
• What is real	• What could be
• Practical	• Theoretical
• Present	• Future
• Facts	• Insights
• Using established skills	• Learning new skills
• Utility	• Novelty
• Step by step	• Leap about

3. Deciding (judgement)

Thinking (T)	Feeling (F)
• Head	• Heart
• Logical system	• Value system
• Objective	• Subjective
• Justice	• Mercy
• Critique	• Compliment
• Principles	• Harmony
• Reason	• Empathy
• Firm but fair	• Compassionate

4. Living (orientation to outside

Judgement (J)	Perception (P)
• Planful	• Spontaneous
• Regulate	• Flow
• Control	• Adapt
• Settled	• Tentative
• Run one's life	• Let life happen
• Set goals	• Get data
• Decisive	• Open
• Organized	• Flexible

EXERCISE

Think about yourself and someone with whom you have worked ineffectively—do you differ on any of these four dimensions? What might you have done to work better together? Consider arranging for you and your team to have your types identified.

Knowing others is intelligence;
knowing the self is enlightenment.

Conquering others is power;
conquering the self is strength.

GREAT COACHES KNOW THEMSELVES. PINPOINT AND OVERCOME YOUR EXCUSES FOR FEELING RELUCTANT TO COACH IN SPECIFIC SITUATIONS, SUCH AS:

Your assumed need for complete control.

Fear that the coachee won't like you.

Fear that you might "fail" as a coach.

8

FINDING AND AVOIDING YOUR COACHING BLOCKS

The champagne corks popped as the deal was finally signed. By acquiring Tubs-and-Cones International, Alex's company had completed the largest takeover in its history, and had become the biggest player in the world ice-cream market

Alex was now in charge of the integration effort (Project Genesis) with a full-time team of 12 people. He felt confident that he could perform, with promotion virtually guaranteed. "Senior manager after only 18 months with the company—not bad!" he mused.

He set to work, laying out a punishing schedule for himself and the team. There was much to be done: defining the new management structure, confirming likely cost savings and synergies, reassuring key customers, and double checking the financial implications of the acquisition.

Bob, still Alex's boss, was right to be concerned. He had noticed that Alex had virtually swaggered out of his office with the good news that he had landed the project management role. Alex was being just a bit too eager.

Because the other team members were not available immediately, Alex had used the intervening time to plan the team's activities in great detail. "Hmm..." he thought, "lots of data to be analyzed on this project. I bet we'll also need to commission some market research, feed the information into a computer to identify the relevant market segments, then we can figure out which marketing channels to use for each type of product in each geographic region...."

> A person may be reluctant to coach in certain situations for reasons that are often misguided. For example, a controlling person often claims that he or she never has enough time to invest in coaching. This person rarely delegates and becomes caught in a vicious circle of workaholism. There are ways out of these and other predicaments.

Unfortunately, Alex was not really a marketing expert; yet by the time the people from the Marketing Department joined the team, they found that Alex had mapped out exactly what they should be doing. Although Alex had made mistaken assumptions about the market, his style did not allow them to correct him. The people from Finance and Operations had similar experiences.

So it was with a feeling of impending doom that the team left its first full meeting. Alex had not asked for any of their expert input, and had allocated all their tasks in extreme detail for the next two months. They were right to be worried. In the following weeks, Alex was in "tell" mode most of the time. Moreover, with little team discussion, people found themselves duplicating each other's work, flying off on tangents, and generally becoming demotivated.

The phone on Alex's desk rang from somewhere beneath the piles of papers which had clearly cost the lives of several Amazonian rain forests. "Hello, Alex, it's Bob—could you drop by for a minute? Yes, now." Bob looked up from his desk as Alex walked in. "Alex, I've got some good news and some bad news—which would you like first?"

Alex elected for the good news first, which was that the Acquisition Review Committee had been reasonably pleased with the progress of Alex's team so far. "However," continued Bob, "we're all worried about whether the rest of the work on this project will get done. You used to be regarded as a good coach and manager, but you seem to have slipped into a mode of real micromanagement over the last month. Several of your team members have even asked to be moved off your team. If you're going to turn into a 'people-eater' there's no way you will be able to manage *this* project. What's gone wrong?"

"There's just not enough time to coach people on this project," shrugged Alex, who went on to explain all the problems which needed to be addressed. "In addition," he continued, "with only three more months for this project to run, I really don't think that any time I invest in coaching now will generate a major benefit."

Bob disagreed. "You have hit a coaching block, Alex. You'll have to overcome it—and fast." Bob went on to explain that managers sometimes run into situations where they feel reluctant to coach. The block most frequently encountered is where the manager says, "There just isn't enough time to coach or to provide feedback." However, this is normally an excuse for "I need to be in complete control—I cannot risk delegating." Clearly, there are times when this response may be appropriate. But too often these situations are exactly the ones in which the manager needs to do everything possible to unleash the full power of the people with whom she/he is working.

"Well, how do I get around this block...and what are the other types of coaching block?" asked Alex.

> **Overcome your coaching blocks, or you'll never delegate.**

"You're good at planning—why not plan some *coaching?*" Bob replied, handing Alex a brief note (reproduced on pages 56 and 57). "I really want you to work on your people skills, Alex. You're strong in all other dimensions of management, but this could really hold you back," he added.

Deep down, Alex knew he'd have to do some serious self-examination—other aspects of his life were not going well. For example, over the preceding few months, his relationship with his girlfriend Rachel had become very strained. She had accused him of never listening to her, and of always trying to organize everything. He had even insisted on telling her exactly what birthday present she should give her mother. The end had come last week when she eventually left him, and returned to an old flame. Perhaps he had become a control freak after all.

Late that night he called Sarah for advice. She was on temporary assignment in Hong Kong, and the difference between time zones meant that she would now be at the office.

Briggs thought he was the best syndicate
accounts manager, data analyst, economist,
underwriter and plate spinner Finklestein,
Hooch & Krupp had ever employed.

WORKING AROUND COACHING BLOCKS

Sometimes we do not take up opportunities to coach other people, even though we are well-intentioned. Why is this, and what can we do about it?

A major organization recently conducted research in this area. It compared the coaching behavior of 80 managers with their in-depth psychological profiles. This identified: (1) four typical rationales that the managers sometimes used to **allow** themselves not to coach; (2) the real underlying reasons for not coaching; and (3) how they could overcome these blocks (see the facing chart).

For example, those managers who claimed they did not have enough time to coach were typically people with an unusually high need to control their environment and the people around them.

While the origins of this trait were buried somewhere in the managers' psychology, the exact cause was irrelevant. The important observation was that, for those managers, the best route into coaching was to control how and when they would provide coaching and feedback.

There were three other frequently encountered coaching blocks, each with its own likely remedy, as shown on the opposite page.

COACHING BLOCKS AND WAYS AROUND THEM

Typical "Rational" for Not Coaching	Possible "Real" Reason	Possible Entry into Coaching
1 "Not enough time to coach."	"I need to be in complete control."	Agree very specifically when and how coaching will happen.
2 "Coachee won't respond, anyway."	"I'm frightened, I can't do it."	Ask coachee how she/he would like to receive feedback/coaching.
3 "The task won't suffer if I don't coach."	"If I ignore it, the problem will go away."	Reassess your ability to become a true leader.
4 "I might hurt them."	"They won't like me."	Start where it is safe—someone with whom you get on well, or someone who is good, but could be great.

EXERCISE

Think back to the last time you should have coached or given feedback. Why didn't you? What would have made it easier for you? See Appendix 6, page 142.

THE "INSTANT PAYOFF" COACHING TECHNIQUE
WILL ALLOW YOU TO HELP YOURSELF AND
OTHERS WHEN TIME IS LIMITED.

1 Define the problem.

2 Visualize the ideal outcome.

3 Identify—and brainstorm around—
the obstacles.

9

COACHING
IN A HURRY

Following his discussion with Bob, Alex had set himself the aspiration of overcoming his coaching block, and so unleashing the team's full potential. He was determined not to be a "control freak" from now on!

Nevertheless, he did know more about the ice-cream industry than anyone else in the company. Very soon, the temptation was too strong. Six weeks later, Alex still found himself suffering from his inability to let go of any part of Project Genesis. Things came to a head halfway through the grueling schedule which Alex had set for integrating the European manufacturing operations of the newly created ice-cream empire.

Most of the joint manufacturing operations were in France, and Alex had thought that Tom (who had continued to work with Alex on Project Genesis, after the original Project Quest) could carry out the interviews there. Alex would go along to the first few interviews, then Tom could carry on by himself, while Alex spent more time on the marketing strategy.

Unfortunately, Alex had early on come to the conclusion that Tom could not do the interviews by himself. Rather than cancel the planned meetings, Alex had handled them all himself, writing up the meeting notes late into the night, then spending an hour or two on the marketing strategy.

One particular night, he had a bad dream: he was doomed to be on a very long project which involved interviewing everyone in the phone book whose telephone number was a prime number. It took a whole year to do this, by which time a new phone book had been published....

Alex was working too hard, and he knew it. He went to see Bob, his boss. "We've got a real problem on the European integration, Bob. We need to renegotiate the timetable."

Bob knew that it would be impossible to change the timetable: everything had to be ready for the peak sales of ice cream next summer. He also did not want to volunteer more of his own time to the project, because of his other commitments. He had to help Alex build his confidence that there were other ways forward, but he was due to get in a cab to the airport in ten minutes.

"What's the problem?" he asked, remembering the instant payoff coaching technique that he had recently picked up from the new company-wide coaching program.

"Well," Alex began, "Tom really isn't skilled at interviewing, and I'm nervous about the reaction to him of our new French subsidiary. I can't see how I can help him, as well as manage the overall project, as well as complete my own work on the marketing strategy...it's simply too much. Given the enormous value of this project to the company, surely we can get agreement to adding another team member—just for a month or two?"

Bob paused before responding. He thought that there might be a better solution—one that would encourage Alex to be less of a control freak. "Let's explore the issue more fully. Tell me what you would see if the problem was fixed; don't tell me how we could do it, just tell me what success would look like."

Alex reflected for a moment. "Well, Tom would have completed all the interviews, would have built relationships with the key executives in France, and would have drafted a report summarizing his findings, which I could discuss with him a few days before the next steering group meeting...."

Alex looked visibly relieved but then panicked, "But he isn't good enough, he..." Bob stopped him. "Before we examine Tom's abilities, tell me the obstacles between where we are now and where you said you'd like us to be."

> Instant payoff coaching can help someone resolve a problem in a limited period of time—for example, in 10–15 minutes. The technique focuses on first envisioning what the successful outcome would look or feel like. Subsequent discussion focuses on identifying the source of constraints or blocks to effective action, and how to deal with them.

As Alex spoke, Bob simply listed the points on a flipchart. He didn't comment on the obstacles, but just asked Alex to look at the completed list, and to indicate where each obstacle lay—in himself, in someone else or in the situation.

Alex was surprised to see how many of the obstacles were in fact to do with himself, and that relatively few were to do with Tom's abilities. Bob didn't need to ask Alex what he was going to focus on as a next step; Alex volunteered. "This is great. I can see a way through this without more people, if you would talk to the Chief Executive of the French subsidiary about his people's dismissive attitudes to Tom. We'll send Tom on a one-day interviewing course, and I'll see if I can come off the recruiting taskforce for just a couple of days." As they ended their ten-minute session, Bob went off to the airport and Alex went down the hall to find Tom.

Thereafter, Alex made great use of the instant payoff coaching technique which he had learned from Bob.

Ted's inability to distinguish giving advice
from delivering criticism holds up the project
at an important stage...

INSTANT PAYOFF COACHING

Sometimes you do not have the time or knowledge to complete a full coaching discussion and really build someone's skills, but you do want to help someone who is "stuck" to complete the task in question.

Using the model shown on the opposite page, you can achieve this in as little as five minutes by helping your coachees to see that they too have some responsibility for the situation and that there is something they can do, however small.

EXERCISE

Try the Instant Payoff Coaching exercise on yourself. If it works, try it with the next person who asks for your advice.

INSTANT PAYOFF COACHING

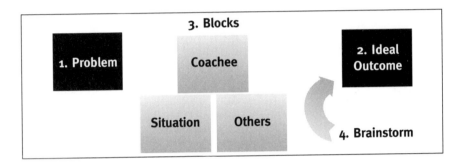

1   Ask the coachee to describe the current issue or problem, with specific examples and a small amount of relevant background.

2   Ask her/him to describe the outcome—paint as specific a picture as possible of how things would be if she/he had sorted out the problem. Do not try to solve the problem, but note down any emerging ideas.

3   With the coachee, list all the obstacles/blocks that lie between 1 and 2. Sort them into three groups:

   • Blocks that exist in the coachee (lack of skill/knowledge, low motivation, attitude, etc.)

   • Blocks that exist in others (anxious customer, manager stressed and panicking, etc.)

   • Blocks in the situation (inadequate resources, shift in deadlines, etc.).

4   Jointly brainstorm ways around these blocks, and possible next steps. Agree on approach, actions, and timing.

Deal with things before they arise.
Cultivate order before confusion sets in.

YOU CAN DELEGATE MORE (AND AVOID UNPLEASANT SURPRISES) BY EXPLICITLY THINKING THROUGH HOW TO ASSIGN AND FOLLOW-UP.

Explicitly diagnose your coachee's skill and will to perform the task at hand.

Adopt the appropriate coaching/management style, using the skill/will matrix.

Modify your style as your coachee makes progress.

10 TAKING ACCOUNT OF OTHERS' SKILL AND WILL

"About time, too," thought Alex, as Bob gave him the official news of his promotion to senior manager.

"Of course," added Bob, reading Alex's mind, "you would have been promoted earlier—based on the project management skills you displayed by completing Project Genesis on time. But we had to be sure that you had the *people* skills needed at senior manager level. We had to be sure that you didn't stumble over your coaching block. After all, inventories can be managed, but people need to be led."

Now, two years into his career with the company, Alex had five or six major initiatives to look after. He knew that in his new role he would have to be careful about how he allocated his time—there really was no way in which he could micromanage all these initiatives at the same time. Fortunately, having seen the power of effective coaching, he had read up on the subject. This was the perfect opportunity to apply the Skill/Will matrix, and he reread the paragraphs from his coaching book.

> In some ways, the idea of the Skill/Will matrix is simple, but it needs practice to apply it effectively. The overall concept is that you tailor your style of coaching and management to the skill and will of the person you are managing, bearing in mind the task they are trying to accomplish.

For example, if someone is able to accomplish a given task, and they are motivated to complete it (that is, high skill and high will), then the appropriate management style would be to Delegate.

However, if the person had low skill and low will—for the task in question—then you would need to be more Directive, at least initially. For high skill, low will—or vice versa—the manager should use Excite or Guide styles respectively.*

While this sounds simple in theory, there are two main challenges. First, you have to really diagnose the coachee's skill and will, without leaping to conclusions based on prejudice or accepting the coachee's frequent pretense to be 'high skill and high will' at everything. And second, you need to modify dynamically your management or coaching style, as the coachee builds both skill and will.

Alex thought about Tom, who had now been with the company for about a year. Tom was in charge of the project to identify the company's next acquisition in the frozen food market. Alex knew that Tom was high on will: he was very enthusiastic about this role, having dropped enough hints to Alex that he wanted the assignment.

But Alex wasn't so sure about Tom's skill. Tom certainly had the creativity and flexibility which the new project might require. But Alex thought Tom was less strong in strategy and valuation analysis.

Rather than leaping to conclusions, however, Alex decided to have a frank discussion with Tom. He was careful to use genuinely open—as opposed to leading—questions, and to avoid an accusing tone of voice. This discussion confirmed Alex's initial thoughts, although he was relieved to discover that Tom had carried out several company valuations while with his previous employer.

"High will, fairly high skill," thought Alex. "I can afford to Delegate and be fairly hands-off; but I had better make sure I provide a bit of Guidance in the area of strategy."

See Appendix 7 (page 144) for descriptions of these styles.

Alex went through a similar process with the four other people who reported directly to him . . . one more Guide, two Delegates and a Direct. He felt relieved that he had things in perspective, and that he could now prioritize his time for the next month or so. Thereafter he'd review progress to see whether he could use more of the Delegate style, to free up more time for himself!

Dr. Frankenstein makes a fundamental error

in his "Jump for Joy" program.

SELECTING AN APPROPRIATE COACHING STYLE: THE SKILL/WILL MATRIX

All too often, we assign a task to someone and the job does not quite get done well enough. Why is this?

One of the most likely reasons is that we have delegated the task to someone who is unwilling—or unable—to complete the job, and have then remained relatively "hands-off" or uninvolved. Alternatively, we may have been "hands-on" or directive with a capable person who was quite able to complete the assignment with little assistance from us; we just ended up demotivating her/him.

Consequently, whether you are "coaching" or just "managing" it is critical to match your style of interaction with the coachee's readiness for the task.

To help you do this, use the Skill/Will matrix:

First, diagnose the coachee's skill and will to accomplish the task, as indicated on the opposite page.

Then use the matrix to identify the appropriate style of interaction— for example, you would want to use Delegate if your coachee was high in both skill and will.

Finally, agree with your coachee which style you will be using and for what reasons.

A few observations:

Ensure you are addressing the coachee's skill and will to execute the specific task in question—for example, "making presentations to the Board of Directors" rather than "public speaking."

If you are working with someone over a longer period, you will want them to increase in both will and skill. If they are successful in doing this, you will need gradually to adopt the appropriate styles en route to Delegate.

(The Skill/Will matrix is an adaptation by Keilty, Goldsmith & Co, Inc., of original work by Hersey and Blanchard.)

USING THE SKILL/WILL MATRIX

1 Diagnose whether the coachee's skill and will are high or low, for the specific task to be accomplished:

Skill depends on experience, training, understanding, role perception

Will depends on desire to achieve, incentives, security, confidence.

2 Identify the appropriate coaching/management style—e.g., use "Guide" if the coachee has high will but low skill for the task.

3 Agree on your intended approach with your coachee.

Skill/Will Matrix

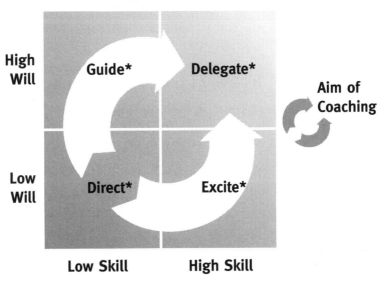

High Will   Guide*   Delegate*   Aim of Coaching

Low Will   Direct*   Excite*

Low Skill   High Skill

> EXERCISE
>
> **Recall a time when you were poorly coached or managed. Was your manager's style consistent with your skill and will? Reflect on your current approach to managing someone else. Do steps 1–3 above suggest any changes?**

* See Appendix 7 (page 144) for details of each approach.

The wise person acts without effort
and teaches by quiet example;
accomplishes without taking credit.

YOU CAN NORMALLY CONVERT A RELUCTANT

COACHEE INTO AN AVID ONE IF

YOU BUILD TRUST...

Trust in you.

Trust in the organization.

11 OVERCOMING A RELUCTANCE TO BEING COACHED

Alex was muttering to himself as he walked down the corridor. Just when he had really begun to master some of the more advanced aspects of coaching, such as the Skill/Will matrix, he had had to endure yet another frustrating and unproductive discussion with Angus, the analyst who was working for Tom on the latest acquisition.

Despite the overwhelming temptation to blame Angus, Alex decided to be more constructive. Applying some self-coaching, he tried the GROW model (refer back to Chapter 6) on himself. "What is my *goal* here...to decide on one thing which might unlock my communication with Angus, so that I can deliver some vital feedback. What about the current *reality*, then..." Alex began to recall his encounter with Angus.

"Angus, how are you doing?" Alex had asked as he had entered Angus's office.

"Fine," had come the rather clipped response.

"Is there anything you would like my help on, while Tom is away on vacation?" In response to the shaken head, Alex had persevered, "Are you absolutely sure that everything is under control—everything which you had agreed with Tom?"

"Absolutely."

Tom had warned Alex that Angus tended to overestimate his ability and that he was reluctant to ask for help. Tom had attributed this to the culture of Angus's previous company, where survival had depended on a continuous show of strength.

Alex offered Angus a chance. "You *are* allowed to ask for help around here, you know." Angus thanked him for the offer, promised to ask for help if needed, and pressed on with his work. As he reflected on the encounter, Alex was puzzled. Surely people knew that they could be open with him.

Build genuine trust with a reluctant coachee.

He thought back to the times when he had been in Angus's situation. As a more junior person, even Alex had been reluctant to disclose his own needs in new relationships with bosses and peers. He had felt that his admissions might just be used against him. Alex realized that—in discussions with Angus—he had been relying purely on his reputation as a good coach. Perhaps Angus did not trust him.

"So," thought Alex, "if trust is the key, what are my *options*? Let's see: (1) tell him it's OK, (2) ask someone else to tell him that I can be trusted, (3) let Tom worry about it...." None of the ideas seemed a likely winner. "All right," he mused, "how do I assess whether I can trust someone?"

As he was jotting down his thoughts he suddenly remembered a simple idea that he had once read about. This was that you could look at a relationship in terms of an "emotional bank account," or how much credit (or debit) of goodwill existed between the two people. With strangers, for example, you might have no store of goodwill, and so it would naturally be difficult to get them to do something for you, since there was no reserve of goodwill upon which to draw.

Alex realized that his emotional bank account with Angus was probably overdrawn. Alex had recently made some last-minute requests of the team, which had made for some long hours. He also recalled that Angus's father—who lived three hours' drive away—was extremely unwell, and that the weekend working made visits difficult. He also realized that he didn't know very much about Angus's aspirations for himself. It now seemed obvious to Alex that the problem lay not so much in his lacking skills as a coach, but rather in his lacking any real relationship with Angus. Having reviewed his options, Alex *wrapped up*; he knew what to do next.

He found out more about Angus from reading through his last annual performance review. He made sure that Angus could get home on the following weekend. And he persuaded Angus to go out for a quick drink with him, during which Alex talked about his own career with the company, how he had found it hard to trust new bosses at first, and how difficult it had been to overcome his doubts. He listened carefully to Angus's description of his previous company, and to his fears and aspirations for the job he was now in.

When Alex felt that the moment was right, he asked Angus how he would like to receive feedback or guidance in the future, should the opportunity arise. He stressed that he meant informal, on-the-job feedback, not the kind that ends up in personnel files. With a more open, trusting relationship, it was easy for Angus to ask for the support he wanted, and he was even willing to ask for Alex and Tom to monitor more closely tasks which were new to him or of particularly high risk.

Alex reflected that perhaps the foundation of all successful coaching is an open, trusting relationship with a healthy reservoir of goodwill on both sides.

Doc Gilby, the Dentist, gained trust and built
confidence through his use of Fluffywuffy the
hand puppet...of course if that didn't work,
there was always Mr. Slap Hammer...

DEALING WITH A COACHEE'S RELUCTANCE TO BE COACHED

You may feel that someone would benefit from your coaching, but that she/he appears reluctant to accept your help.

To make progress, you will need to diagnose why the potential coachee is resisting you. He or she may be reluctant to accept any form of coaching by anyone, or may just be reluctant to have **you** as a coach at the current time.

To take appropriate initiatives, you will need to proceed to at least one further level of diagnosis (see opposite page).

EXERCISE

Identify your most "reluctant" coachee. Develop a plan using the above pointers.

DEALING WITH RELUCTANCE

Coachee's mindset	Options for the coach
Intrinsic reluctance to be coached	
• Unwillingness to admit room for improvement (in general or in the specific coaching topic)	• Diagnose the coachee's barriers • Emphasize factual evidence for the need to improve ("push" strategy) or... • Break through by asking the coachee to coach you ("pull" strategy)
• Mistrust of the organization	• Build the trust
• Temporary lack of available time	• Agree to a later session
Reluctance to be coached by you	
• Unhelpful historical relationship with you	• Attempt to "bury the hatchet"*
• Major difference between her /his style and yours	• Discuss explicitly, and accept, the "style" differences if possible* (see Chapter 7)
• Perceived nature of your role in the organization as being highly evaluative	• Be explicit about your role— e.g., whether you determine the coachee's remuneration • Stress that the coaching is nonevaluative*

*Or suggest an alternative coach if all else fails

Guide others by quietly relying on Tao.
Then, when the work is done, the people can say,
"We did this ourselves."

SHIFT YOUR COACHEE TO A POSITIVE CYCLE OF CONFIDENCE FROM A NEGATIVE CYCLE OF HESITANCY OR CONCERN BY KNOWING HOW TO MOTIVATE.

Understand specifically what factors motivate your coachee in relevant situations.

Work on building self-esteem.

Suggest training or other support if needed.

12 MOTIVATING

A few weeks later, Alex reflected on his two-and-a-half years with the company. He was glad he had joined the firm: he seemed to be well-regarded, had been promoted with reasonable speed, and he admired the people-oriented culture that, he felt sure, had something to do with the company's performance, which exceeded the industry's average.

In his senior manager role he had thought a bit about the topic of motivating others. There didn't seem to be many books on the subject, so he had gradually pieced together tips from watching what other particularly good managers did.

As he thought about Mary—who had joined his division 18 months ago, and for whom he was preparing an end-of-year appraisal session—he wondered how he could apply the three lessons he had learnt about motivation. These were:

(1) *help the coachee to understand consciously her/his current level of motivation;*

(2) *help the coachee to fashion a really convincing vision of how well she/he could perform; and*

(3) *support the coachee in her/his efforts through praise and coaching.*

Alex had spent the first 15 minutes of his meeting with Mary reviewing her performance so far. It had not been easy, since she had been "low skill, low will" on many of her recent assignments. Alex now decided to switch direction for the last 15 minutes of the meeting.

"Mary, it seems to me that you are caught in a negative cycle. You start off lacking confidence in your abilities; this leads you to make hesitant attempts at the tasks on which you are engaged; as a result, you deliver below your real potential; and then you receive less praise than you would hope for. This in turn just exacerbates your lack of confidence." Alex sketched out the cycle. (See page 87.)

"You know, Alex," she responded, "I think you're right. I'd never thought about it this way before; everything just seemed all tangled up. But how can I break out of this cycle into a more positive one?"

> **Motivation is a critical aspect of managing and coaching. Motivational factors, however, differ widely from individual to individual.**

"Let's think about something at which you could be really good... any suggestions?"

They discussed a few options, and discarded some which didn't seem relevant enough to Mary's mainstream work activities. In the end, they decided that Mary was going to become the best person in the entire company at making presentations. Alex thought the objective was stretching, but achievable. Although Mary was a bit shy, she was a key figure in the local amateur drama group.

"Now, how are we going to get there?" asked Alex. Mary had perked up as the result of the preceding discussion, but now gulped and paled. Alex bit his lip and resisted the temptation to dive in and rescue her. Eventually, Mary came up with a surprisingly rich stream of her own ideas, ranging from making the prize draw at the departmental Christmas party to running the induction session for people who were just joining the company.

"And what type of help do you think you need?" probed Alex.

"I think I can handle most of this myself!" responded a reenergized Mary, whose ideas ranged from taking a one-day course in presenting herself with more impact to noting the presentation techniques of famous people as they appeared on television.

"All I'd ask is that you give me some feedback whenever you see me make a presentation."

"What on earth have you done to Mary while I've been away?" It was the long-lost Sarah standing at Alex's door.

Sarah had just returned from her assignment in the company's Hong Kong operation. She had worked with Mary before. But now, several weeks after the annual appraisal session with Alex, Mary seemed a different person.

It turned out that Mary was making real progress in building her presentation skills. But—perhaps more importantly—her growing self-confidence in this area was already spilling over into other areas of her work.

She was indeed becoming a much more motivated person. Alex was beginning to think that the time he had invested during the appraisal session had been well worthwhile, and he was glad that he had not confined himself to merely running through the company's standard appraisal form with Mary.

"Well, how were things in Hong Kong?" inquired Alex. "I tried to call you several times, but you had always just left for some part of Southeast Asia."

"It's a long story," said Sarah. "But I really learned a lot about managing in an environment with a different culture."

You can't motivate others

if they can't see you...

MOTIVATION

The golden rules of motivation:

1 Know where your coachees are in the cycle of motivation or demotivation shown opposite.

2A Work on their confidence, if they are in the uppermost cycle, because it's about the only thing you can affect directly. Do this by:

- Working with them to develop a vision of how good they could be at completing a specific task, or playing a specific role;
- Recognizing that improved performance in an area that might not be critical to their mainstream activities usually has very positive spin-off benefits to their core activities.

2B Work on praise if they are in the lower cycle.

3 Identify their needs for support and/or training, even if it is to be provided by the coachee themselves or by a third party.

4 Know what most motivates your coachees. Everyone has different motivating factors (see Appendix 8, page 146).

EXERCISES

Name four people you work with, identify which cycle they are in and whether you can help them do even better.

Have your team complete Appendix 5 (page 139), and compare the results, which will differ surprisingly between respondents.

NEGATIVE CYCLE OF DEMOTIVATION

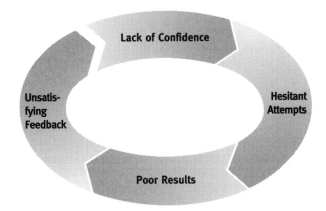

POSITIVE CYCLE OF DEMOTIVATION

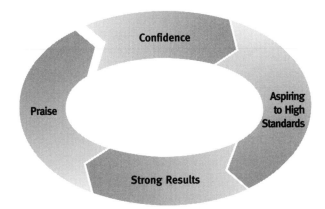

The great country wants to embrace and nourish more people.
The small country wants to ably serve its benefactor.
Both accomplish their ends by yielding.

TO GET THE MOST OUT OF MULTINATIONAL TEAMS,

RECOGNIZE AND RESPECT CULTURAL

DIFFERENCES. KNOW HOW TO USE:

Directness

Hierarchy

Consensus

13

RECOGNIZING CULTURAL DIFFERENCES

Alex found himself pinned to his seat as flight MA245 took off, ultimate destination Moravia, via Paris. Project Genesis—the integration of Cones-and-Tubs into the company—was nearing completion, but the company had just completed a further acquisition to make it the largest ice-cream producer in Eastern Europe.

The following morning he found himself in the boardroom of the new Moravian subsidiary, ready for his first full meeting with the local management team. Alex knew the meeting was critical, and knew that it would not be easy to manage this far-flung arm of the company from New York. So he had to take every opportunity to build the credibility of the head office as soon as possible.

Consequently, he had decided to have dinner with the local Strategy Director, Jan, the previous evening to agree how they would run the management meeting. Jan would start off with the agreed presentation on the benefits of the merger, then there would be a free-format discussion, followed by a tour of the plant. Alex had met with Jan only once before, but gained the impression that he was very pushy. So Alex had spent a few minutes gently coaching him on how to soften his style.

Alex cringed as Jan delivered his presentation to the assembled managers. "Oh no," thought Alex, "what a disaster!"

He knew that Moravians typically pulled no punches. They communicated in a very forthright manner. But surely Jan was going too far. What about the coaching session which Alex had had with him the night before?

Why was Jan not using the softer approach which they had discussed? And what had happened to the comments on which they had agreed as face-saving measures for the local chief executive?

Alex searched in vain for a way to intercede as Jan increased the tempo. He felt the perspiration on his brow. "At least," he thought, "I know how frank to be in my feedback to Jan as soon as this meeting is over!"

Perhaps it was the pressure, perhaps it was the local Moravian brew he had consumed the night before, perhaps it was the jet lag, but Alex seemed to lose touch with reality for what seemed like only an instant. The next thing he knew, the audience was on its feet—a standing ovation!

Later that day, Alex reflected on how he might have managed things differently. Although things had worked out OK in the end, Alex concluded that he'd be more careful next time he coached someone from an obviously different culture. He would think in advance about the most important cultural differences between himself, the coachee, and the coaching context.

For example, Alex thought he should have listened more to Jan over dinner, perhaps discussing openly the cultural issues relating to the forthcoming meeting—rather than presumptuously coaching him on how to soften his style. Nevertheless, if Alex did have to coach Jan again, he would probably be much more frank in his advice, to match Jan's cultural background.

Furthermore, Jan—like Alex—was used to operating in an environment without much hierarchy. However, if Jan had typically been more deferential to his bosses, Alex reflected that he would have had to exercise care that a brainstormed idea was not interpreted as a direct order.

Similarly, the meaning—and importance—of teamwork can differ significantly or subtly between cultures, with implications for the senior manager who is attempting to build a team.

Alex boarded the Boeing 727 that would take him home. He was glad that he'd decided to stop over in Paris for the weekend, and was even more delighted to have discovered that Sarah would be there too. He wanted to discuss her experiences in Hong Kong, and compare notes on how to be an effective manager in an unfamiliar culture.

Although Friday afternoon "Postboy Racing" had been a popular pastime where Lars came from, he still had quite a bit to learn about Frimly and Booth office culture...

CULTURAL DIFFERENCES

When coaching someone from a different culture, she/he may well act—or react—differently from what you are used to:

Cultural differences do not arise only from national, racial or religious origins—for example, people new to your organization may still be heavily influenced by the culture of their previous employer.

These differences can result in higher or lower levels of perceived performance, and in more or less need for—and acceptance of—feedback.

When working with multinational teams, or individuals from cultures different from yours, be explicit with yourself, and ideally with them, about the implications of cultural differences.

Above all, commit to building shared expectations—in terms of management style, adherence to deadlines, frequency of progress checks, need for creativity, etc.

For further details, see **Cultures and Organizations** by Geert Hofstede.

FOUR CULTURAL DIMENSIONS

Cultures—both national and organizational—differ along many dimensions. Four of the most important ones are indicated below:

Dimension	Implication for the coach
Directness (get to the point versus imply the messages)	Tailor style of feedback appropriately.
Hierarchy (follow orders versus engage in debate)	Position coaching relationship carefully vis à vis organizational reporting relationship.
Consensus (dissent is accepted versus unanimity is needed)	Select from full repertoire of ask/tell styles—see pages 10 and 11.
Individualism (individual winners versus team effectiveness)	Reflect on focus of coaching—e.g., whether or not to focus on teamwork.

EXERCISE
Recall the last time you had difficulty working with someone from another culture. What went wrong? Why? Could you have avoided the problem? Would it have been worth doing?

In leadership, be organized.
In work, do your best. In action, be timely.

A WELL-DEFINED WORKING APPROACH IS ESSENTIAL
FOR EFFECTIVE TEAMWORK AND FOR A POSITIVE
COACHING ENVIRONMENT. MAKE SURE YOU HAVE:

An organized kickoff meeting.

A clear personal agenda
(including coach/manager).

An open discussion of team
dynamics.

14 STARTING TEAMS WELL

By the time Alex turned up at the party to celebrate Sarah's promotion, the room was already full. Sarah was both highly popular and widely respected as a manager, so attendance was high.

Glass in hand, Alex squeezed away from the crowded bar, and found space within listening distance of a small group of people. One of them, Tom, had recently joined Alex's task force, which was developing the company's three-year plan, and the others seemed to be quizzing him. Alex eavesdropped attentively from his position behind the potted plant.

"What's it like working with this Alex guy?" asked someone. "I hear he sets a pretty punishing schedule, and I know he used to be a real people-eater."

"I think that's a thing of the past," replied Tom. "We just had a kick-off meeting on this planning task force of his, and I must say that Alex really seems to be a good people manager as well as being smart."

"How do you mean?"

"Well, he had set the meeting up really well. There are five of us on this task force, and he'd sent us all a copy of the work plan which he'd drafted, several days in advance."

"What's the big deal about that?" asked another member of the group.

"The point is, he made it very clear that he'd welcome our comments on the plan," Tom continued. "He must have done a bit of research on each of us, too—even the people brought in from other departments—because he sort of knew which areas each of us could best comment on."

"Anyway, we got together for the meeting, and he gave a really convincing speech about the importance of the work—he managed to build a genuine spirit of camaraderie."

"And then he handed out copies of the last annual appraisal which his boss had given him—not just the good stuff, but the things that he needs to improve."

"But why on earth did he do that?" asked someone else.

"Well, he didn't tell us why in so many words, but the effect was quite powerful, because it made people really open up when he asked each of us to explain what we wanted personally to get out of this project. And we really believed him when he said that this was going to be a team in which we gave each other a lot of feedback, and helped each other out if we needed to."

"We even spent five minutes on which parts of the project looked the most busy, to check that the inevitable late hours weren't going to interfere too much with our personal lives."

"Then we talked through our roles and responsibilities. You know, he actually listened to what we had to say, and we rearranged that draft work plan quite a bit. When we left the meeting, we all knew pretty much what we were meant to do, and felt that this was going to be a real team effort. We even agreed to have a team appraisal session in three weeks' time, to check that our teamwork was up to par." (See Appendix 9 on page 149.)

"You don't need a Ph.D. in rocket science to do that kind of thing," quipped a more cynical bystander.

"No, you don't," replied Tom, "but tell me if you've ever had a team meeting like that. And that thing about sharing his own annual appraisal—

the only reason it had impact was that it took some courage on his part."Alex could not suppress a self-contented smirk as he sidled away to find Sarah. "So that was what 'corridor talk' sounded like first hand...!" he thought. "And it's true, you don't necessarily need to be a rocket scientist to be a great team leader."

He also thought about how valuable his skills in one-to-one coaching had been when it came to building and managing a team.

As Dr. Peterson and Professor Forbes
slug it out over who has first use of the
Nobo board, the rest of the U.N. Peace
Mission start laying odds...

COACHING IN THE TEAM CONTEXT

Some teams work hard, have fun and get the job done. Other teams are miserable and ineffective, despite the fact that all the team members are working twice as hard as normal. Why is this?

In their book **The Wisdom of Teams**, Jon Katzenbach and Douglas Smith identified the six basic requirements for good teamwork illustrated below. While it is beyond our scope to address each of these basics, let's review the one most related to coaching—the well-defined working approach.

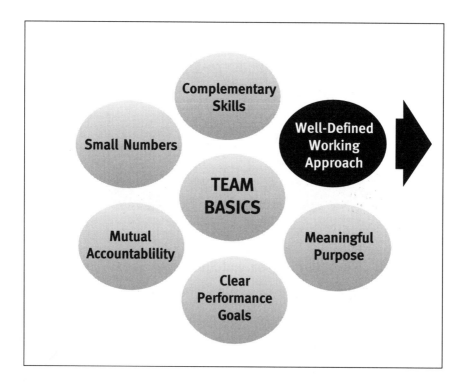

DEFINE YOUR APPROACH

A well-defined working approach is integral to effective teamwork and essential for a positive coaching environment.

Constructive characteristics include:

1 The leader holds a half-day meeting within the first two weeks, to agree on ground rules and "team charter"—for example,
   • Individuals' objectives.
   • Working hours and likely "crunch" periods.

2 Individuals discuss personal needs for skills development openly and early.
   • Set example by sharing last personal performance review with team.
   • Set clear expectations for feedback.

3 The whole team participates in drafting workplan.

4 All team members feel comfortable providing and receiving ongoing feedback and "blowing the whistle" if necessary.

5 The team reviews how it is working every six weeks, or more frequently if needed, or after major milestones (e.g., after publishing a report).

> ### EXERCISE
> **Consider points 1–5 in the context of your current project and suggest/take corrective action if needed.**

Attain your purpose,
but don't press your advantage.
Be resolute, but don't boast.
Succeed, but don't crow.
Accomplish, but don't overpower.

AS YOU COACH, BE CAREFUL TO:

Focus on the practical and observable; don't become too psychological.

Remember that decisive action—not coaching—is sometimes needed.

15 Coaching Caveats

Alex had just been on a long vacation, to celebrate his fourth anniversary with the company. He had returned with a tan and a general feeling of well-being—particularly since his relationship with his new girlfriend had endured its first holiday test.

He ploughed through his in-tray with the help of his secretary, and as she was leaving he asked her for an update on the rumor, scandal and gossip from the office grapevine.

"Not much to report," she began, "It's been pretty quiet. All I've really heard is that Tim and Mary have had a blow-up."

Mary was one of Alex's most able managers. She was spending a lot of time with Tim, from the marketing department, on a taskforce to revamp the company's research and development process. Although progress had been excellent, Alex had noticed that there had been some friction between the two of them.

"Time for a coaching session," thought Alex, recalling the GROW framework which he had used so successfully over the years.

He met with Mary and they agreed that teamwork would be a good topic to discuss.

"How are you getting along with Tim?" asked Alex.

"Not too well," responded Mary, "we just don't seem to be on the same wavelength."

Mary thought for a moment. "Actually, we get along OK when there are just two of us. The friction seems to arise when there are other people in the room."

Alex was sure he knew what was happening. He'd noticed that Mary had been very competitive in the company's recent annual softball tournament. Mary's problems with Tim conveniently confirmed Alex's hypothesis that she felt a need to assert herself when the audience grew larger than one.

"Do you sometimes feel a need to prove yourself in meetings with Tim, particularly when there are other people present?" Alex knew he was taking a chance, but he had a strong hunch that he was on the right track.

Mary looked suspiciously at Alex. "Well, er...no, not really."

"And did you feel competitive towards your brother when you were younger?" Alex continued.

Now Mary was *really* beginning to wonder what was happening. She glanced nervously around the room, noticing as she did so several well-thumbed books by Freud lying on the bookshelf. "Actually," Mary replied politely, "I've always got on very well with my family."

Alex pursued the point for a few more minutes until a call from overseas interrupted their meeting. It was Mary's chance to escape from the amateur psychologist's couch, and she took it.

Within a few days, Mary had resolved her problem with Tim. When Alex noticed the change he had a chat with Mary, and was surprised to find that their problems had arisen purely from a few specific misunderstandings. Then he thought back to his ineffective coaching session, and realized that he might have missed the point.

Perhaps it was inappropriate to delve too deeply into psychology. "A little learning is a dangerous thing..." he mused. Next time he would listen more, and focus on the facts of the situation, taking them more at face value.

However, Alex had another problem which he was to discover the next day, and which would take several months of hard work to sort out. In the period prior to his vacation he had spent so much time on coaching, motivating and feeding back to people that he had taken his eye off the underlying business issues. Some tough decisions had been called for. But rather than take those decisions himself, he had delegated them to his teams. "After all," he had thought, "my teams are empowered." But unfortunately he had over-delegated the process of resolving several important strategic issues.

**Armed to the teeth with his sixth sense
and no flashlight, Ted presses on.**

COACHING CAVEATS

When helping to build skills, great coaches—in contrast to great psychologists—typically do not delve deeply into the coachee's psyche.

They work with, and provide feedback on, perceived behaviors and actions.

By way of analogy, we know how to switch channels on a TV set without knowing the details of the circuits inside. Consequently, bear in mind the overall guidelines for coaching indicated on the opposite page.

Furthermore, the skilled business manager—unlike the "empowerment gone-mad" coach—knows where to inject a dose of firm decision-making.

1 Don't become too "psychological."

Do	Don't
Focus on helping the coachee with specific tasks	Search for psychological problems which might exist
Be businesslike and frank	Try to be nice
Check that you are addressing a real issue	Miss the point
Moderate the amount anddepth of your coaching	Overcoach
Refer people with major personal problems to a qualified counselor	Bite off more than you can chew

2 Don't lose sight of strategic and operational issues which need your decisive action.

One who wishes to guide the people
should be humble in her speech toward them.

One who wishes to lead the people
must learn the art of following them.

GIVING FEEDBACK TO YOUR BOSS CAN BUILD YOUR RELATIONSHIP, AND CAN BE REWARDING, IF DONE CAREFULLY.

Most bosses welcome feedback—if it
is well intended.

Position your offer to provide
feedback sensitively.

16 GIVING FEEDBACK UPWARDS

Alex had eventually resolved those strategic issues which he had let slip several months ago. But, with only six weeks to go until the shareholders' Annual General Meeting, he was growing nervous.

He was supposed to be helping Peter, the Chairman, with his speech, but whenever they met they always seemed to end up wasting a lot of time. First, Peter was rather disorganized and took ages to retrieve relevant papers from accidental hiding places. Second, people who happened to be passing Peter's office tended to just drop by and interrupt their meetings.

"Boy," thought Alex as the fourth person in as many minutes knocked on the door, "Peter could really use some feedback and coaching on time management and personal organization. I wonder if anyone has ever mentioned anything to him in the past."

As their meeting eventually drew to a close, Alex moved towards the door, plucked up courage, and turned to Peter. "By the way, the company-wide coaching program which we launched several years ago seems to be going really well. In fact, I've found the upward feedback which I've received has been very helpful—not just soft stuff, but suggestions that have really increased my effectiveness. How have you found it?"

"I must admit I haven't really had time to ask for any feedback, although I know the program is meant to be for everyone."

Alex paused in case Peter felt like inviting him to share his observations, but he waited in vain. He took a slightly deeper breath than normal and feigned nonchalance. "Of course, we could just take a few minutes at the end of our next meeting if you'd like any suggestions from me," he volunteered. The Chairman was apparently receptive, and Alex made a mental note to gather his thoughts prior to next week's rendezvous.

As that next meeting ended, Alex braced himself. "Well," he began, "how about that upward feedback?"

"I'm not sure I've got time for a discussion now," replied Peter.

"But perhaps there are ways for you to actually create more time for yourself," continued Alex undaunted. "I've been giving it some thought." The Chairman looked up, surprised but intrigued.

Alex said that he had a few ideas which might be helpful, but decided (remembering to use his full repertoire of ask/tell styles) to ask Peter what he thought would be the most useful area to cover. Peter was definitely interested in the topic of time management.

Alex suggested that they focus on the 45-minute meeting which they had just concluded, to see whether there were any clues to greater effectiveness.

After some discussion, Peter volunteered that he really should have his secretary set up a better filing system; that way he wouldn't spend ages looking for lost papers. They also brainstormed a further 20 ideas, all of which had some merit.

Just when Peter thought they had finished the discussion, Alex decided to broach what he was afraid would be the most sensitive area. He knew that Peter liked to maintain a strict "open-door policy," but Alex was sure that the frequent interruptions which had frustrated him during the last three-quarters of an hour probably continued all day.

"Just a final thought, Peter; how about asking your secretary to screen out more of the people who drop by on a casual basis? I'm sure that would save you a lot of time, by allowing you to concentrate on one thing at a time. For example, we must have had 15 interruptions in the last 45 minutes. I know you like to have an open-door policy, but there is a difference between the door being ajar and it being agape!"

"Well, Alex, I always like people to feel they can contact me whenever they need to."

"Yes," responded Alex, "but the result is that everyone who has ever met with you (and therefore been interrupted by others) feels entirely at home getting their own back and making up for the time they lost in their original meeting with you, by interrupting the next person you are seeing." Alex realized he was going all out and wondered how Peter would respond.

Peter was genuinely surprised—he had no idea of the dynamic that his open-door policy had set up. However, he balked at the prospect of forgoing his previously enshrined principle.

Having gone this far, Alex was not about to give up. "Why don't you try an experiment for one week, Peter. After all, what's the worst that could happen?"

Peter did try it for a week. It worked, and he suddenly found himself with much more time than he'd ever had.

He went to find Alex. "I just wanted to thank you for the *upward* feedback. That open-door policy worked when I started the company 30 years ago, but now we're a large multinational company. You were right to point out that the door should be *ajar* not agape. Actually, you've prompted me to revamp a number of my other working habits, too."

"Good man, that Alex," muttered the Chairman to himself as he headed off down the corridor.

"I'm glad we had this little chat, Eddie, it turns out you're not the sneaky, sniveling, crying-in-the-toilets type I'd mistaken you for—when you get back to your office, order yourself a new swivel chair like mine..."

ESTABLISHING AN EFFECTIVE ENVIRONMENT FOR UPWARD FEEDBACK

Giving upward feedback is the same as giving feedback downwards, or sideways, to peers provided you establish an explicit contract with your boss to do so.

Most people really appreciate constructive, timely, actionable and sensitively delivered feedback. However, you may sometimes feel that it is more difficult to deliver than it really is.

Creating an environment and relationship which supports mutual giving and receiving of feedback is best done at the beginning of a task or working relationship, before there is any actual feedback to be given.

Useful ways to position the offer:

Would you like to receive feedback? If so, about what in particular, and in what form?

If I have any observations about you that I think might be helpful to you or your team, how would you like me to communicate them?

Is there any part of a specific task on which we are collaborating where feedback from me would be particularly helpful?

It feels nerve-wracking to give feedback to you because you are so busy/tired/preoccupied/focused. How can I best get through to you in these situations?

EXERCISE

At the beginning of your next project at work, agree with your boss how you will handle upward feedback.

Those who are interested in service
act without motive.

BEYOND COACHING, BEING A MENTOR CAN BRING YOU FURTHER BENEFITS FOR LIMITED INVESTMENTS OF TIME.

Effective mentoring can have an in-delible positive impact.

Mentoring is like coaching but is longer-term and addresses broader issues.

Mentors' initiatives range from confi-dence-building to role modeling.

17   Mentoring

With the Annual General Meeting out of the way, Alex had—in addition to his many other roles within the company—resumed his involvement in recruiting. He and several colleagues were discussing a candidate; it was time for the vote. All those who believed that the company should offer Donald the job were to raise their hands. Alex's hand went up, along with everyone else's.

He felt that Donald would be a great addition to the company. Alex thought that he had a few rough edges but that these could be smoothed out fairly easily. Like Alex four years earlier, Donald's first position would be as manager of strategic planning.

A month later, Alex found himself as the official mentor to Donald, in the new company-wide mentoring program. As no one really knew what a mentor was meant to do beyond taking the mentee out for a quick welcoming lunch, Alex decided to go back to first principles in his search for an answer. He thumbed through his dictionary:

Mentor. A guide, a wise friend and counselor. In Homer's Odyssey, Mentor was an old friend of Odysseus to whom the latter entrusted his home and his son Telemachus. The goddess Minerva assumed the form of Mentor to help Telemachus in his search for Odysseus who had left Ithaca for Troy.

"Well what on earth does one do to become a guide, a wise and faithful counselor," he thought, "short of becoming a classical deity?"

Over the next few months, Alex discovered that being a mentor was a lot like being a coach. First, there were times when the mentor could help the mentee to raise her/his spirits—and aspirations. Sometimes this involved using the skills of motivation that Alex had picked up earlier in his career; at other times Alex merely had a discussion that helped Donald to stand back from the problems of the moment, and to see his work and life in a broader context.

Then there were the times when Alex just provided a listening ear. He knew that Donald did not necessarily want Alex to help him with a specific problem, nor to officially voice a concern. Donald merely wanted to get something off his chest and to know that someone senior cared enough to listen.

Sometimes Alex did need to shift into a more hands-on role, helping Donald to think through his options. These discussions normally focused on broader career issues, rather than the more task-specific issues addressed by a coach.

On other occasions, Alex provided information which Donald might not easily have gained from other sources—such as when he explained the company's emerging strategy in East Asia, and how Donald might use his knowledge of Mandarin to further his career.

Finally, there were times when Alex was the only person who would take on the task of advising Donald on a few changes in style which might not go amiss. Like the time when Donald had started to wear green suits with pink shirts and brown shoes: it wasn't against company policy, but it didn't exactly enhance his credibility. And no one else had felt like giving the feedback.

Alex had also learned to avoid playing certain roles which, at first glance, might appear to be part of a mentor's job description. For example, he had become very careful not to wade in with lots of advice. There were times when he was too far removed from the specific facts of a complicated situation to know what the correct answer was. It was then that he focused on helping Donald to come up with his own answers—just as the effective parent helps the child to become a problem-solver rather than a follower of "advice-interpreted-as-orders."

Alex also tried to avoid being a "rescuer." He knew that it would not help Donald in the long run if he took over any of Donald's problems. For example, Donald was having a problem with his boss, who was a close friend of Alex's. It would have been easy for Alex to have a quiet talk with his friend, but he resisted the temptation. He knew that Donald would learn more from figuring out and implementing the answer for himself. Donald would also have more confidence to solve a similar problem next time without having to turn to Alex.

> **Mentoring is a role that includes coaching techniques, but it also embraces broader counseling and support parameters, such as career counseling on a personal level.**

Later, Alex reflected on the time he had spent mentoring Donald. He hadn't spent too many hours on it, but there were certainly other things for which he could have used the time. He concluded that there were some intangible benefits to being a mentor, such as those that Sarah had described in her article in the company magazine several years ago, but that was about it.

Just as Alex was turning his attention to other matters, Donald turned up. "Alex, I've never really thanked you for all your advice. I just want you to know that you have had a real impact on me. You have even helped me indirectly with my relationship with my girlfriend. I'm not sure if you know, but she's the Chairman's daughter, and we're going to get married. I've already told my future father-in-law what a great guy you are."

"Well," thought Alex, "perhaps there is such a thing as divine justice, after all."

Alex cleared his desk, remembering to take with him his hand-held dictating machine, in case he had any unusual ideas while on vacation. He had completed all his preparations for the meeting of the Board which would take place in his absence.

On his way home he picked up the airline tickets that would take him to Greece....

Before the sudden arrival of a coach and
mentor, the young da Vinci felt that his
job was somehow unfulfilling.

MENTORING

Mentoring and coaching are very similar activities. The only real difference is that the coach focuses on building the coachee's ability to accomplish specific tasks, whereas the mentor has a wider perspective. The mentor typically has a longer-term relationship with the mentee, or is a counselor on a broader range of issues at any given time.

There are a number of different mentoring roles you could find yourself playing—as an "official" mentor if your organization has a system for helping recently hired people, or as a longer-term, friendship-based mentor who counsels someone for a significant part of his or her career. Between these two extremes lies a variety of other types of relationship.

However, all mentoring roles use all or most of the seven types of assistance indicated opposite.

EXERCISE

Review your performance as a mentor. Compare your perspectives with those of your mentee(s). See Appendix 10, page 153.

SEVEN TYPES OF MENTORING ASSISTANCE*

Type of Assistance:	How to Do It:
1 Helping the mentee to a positive mental attitude.	See **Motivation,** pages 86 and 87.
2 Listening when the mentee has a problem; identifying the mentee's feelings and legitimizing them.	Provide a listening ear, without a judgemental response. Explore options if appropriate.
3 Providing appropriate information when needed.	See **Providing Feedback,** pages 32 and 33. Mentors also provide access to privileged (but authorized) information.
4 Encouraging exploration of options.	See **GROW,** pages 40 and 41.
5 Delegating tasks and authority.	See **Skill/Will** matrix, pages 70 and 71.
6 Effectively confronting negative behaviors.	See **Providing Feedback,** pages 32 and 33.
7 Providing a role model.	Create opportunities for working together, where needed skills can be demonstrated and assimilated.

*Adapted from **Mentoring,** by Gordon Shea.

The wise person puts himself last,
and thereby finds himself first; holds himself outside,
and thereby remains at the center.

THE EFFECTS OF YOUR COACHING CAN BE
EVEN MORE POWERFUL THAN YOU IMAGINE.

18

REFLECTING ON
COACHING:
A SUMMARY

Settling back into his poolside chair and gazing out over the Aegean once again, Alex came to the end of his career flashback. He reloaded the dictating machine which he had first picked up several hours earlier. "Yes," he thought, "but what does the great coach really do, when we cut through all the frameworks?"

Pausing to collect his thoughts, he refilled his glass with ouzo, reapplied the sunscreen and began to speak into the machine again.

Let's take a working definition of coaching and then identify the skills and habits that characterize the effective coach. Most coaches have ingrained these coaching skills and habits into their daily lives.

Coaching aims to enhance the performance and learning ability of others. It involves providing feedback, but it also uses other techniques such as motivation, effective questioning and consciously matching your management style to each coachee's readiness to undertake a particular task. It is based on helping people to help themselves through interacting dynamically with them—it does not rely on a one-way flow of telling and instructing.

Figure 1 provides a structured list of the activities of the great coach in the workplace. Let's examine them in sequence.

1 **Setting the context.** This is a critical event; too often we dive into providing feedback with no warning. That can leave the coachee feeling gratuitously "judged" and unwilling to accept ideas which she/he might otherwise have accepted.

So good coaches habitually make explicit with the coachee the context for their forthcoming interactions. (Figure 2 provides some examples.) However, the coach needs to do some homework first—particularly if she/he is the coachee's boss. This includes:

Diagnosing the skill and will of the coachee to accomplish the task. Refer back to the Skill/Will matrix on page 71.

Agreeing to the coaching approach. The Skill/Will matrix will suggest the overall coaching approach you will want to take: Directing, Guiding, Exciting or Delegating (pages 144 and 145). However, it is worth being explicit with the coachee about the logistics: How frequently will you provide feedback? What types of coaching sessions will you have? What preparation will you expect of the coachee? You should also make sure you know how your coachees prefer to take in information—by the written word (give them key points in writing), the spoken word (talk to them), visually (illustrate with charts and figures) or by doing (have them work with you in order to practice).

Building trust in the coaching relationship. Effective coaching only really happens when the coachee trusts the coach. This trust may exist from previous interactions you have had with the coachee—or you may need to "earn" it. A powerful way to

Figure 1

THE COACHEE'S GAME PLAN

1 Set the context

Diagnose skill and will

Agree on the approach

Build trust

Motivate

2 Provide ongoing coaching

Use GROW sessions (20–60 minutes)

Provide feedback (actionable, frequent, 5–10 minutes)

Give praise (frequent, where warranted, 1+ minutes)

Illustrate actively

3 Conclude effectively

Encourage coachee to reflect

Elicit feedback for coach

Agree on next steps

do this is to disclose something of your own strengths, weaknesses and experiences. For example, you could share your last performance review with your coachee, or describe relevant situations you have confronted in the past.

Motivating the coachee. Do you know what really motivates the people with whom you work? Try the following exercise: give your colleagues or teammates a copy of pages 146 to 148, amended as you see fit, and share your—and the team's—completed results with them. You will be surprised at the wide variety of responses. Effective motivation requires two things. First, you must know what really excites your coachee about her/his job—why does she/he really come to work in the morning? Second, you will do well to paint an engaging vision of how well your coachee really could perform (Figure 3), building the cycle of confidence explained on page 86.

2   **Providing ongoing guidance.** Once the context is understood and agreed, you're ready for a series of coaching interactions. You will already have agreed how often these discussions will take place and how long they will last. In practice, you are likely to use four types of interaction:

> *Substantive sessions of, say, 20 to 60 minutes based on the GROW structure* (refer back to page 41). If your coaching "contract" extends over two to three months, you may decide to have three such sessions—at the beginning, middle and end of your collaboration. Try to vary the amount of time you spend on the Goal, Reality, Options and Wrap-up, to make the most effective use of your time with the coachee.

> *Brief discussions of five to ten minutes, to provide feedback* in a timely manner, soon after the coachee's actions which you have observed.

Figure 2

WAYS TO MAKE THE CONTEXT EXPLICIT

1 Obtaining coaching

(To boss) "I'm really trying to build my skills in [topic]. I'd be very grateful if you could coach me on this, during our next project. Would you be willing to do this? When would it be convenient to discuss the logistics of that coaching support?"

(To peer) "I've always thought you were really good at [topic]. I'm trying to get better at this myself. Could I seek your advice and coaching on this during the next few months? Perhaps we could meet for 30 minutes on Friday afternoons/over lunch/over a drink on the occasional evening?"

(To more junior person) "I'd really appreciate your feedback and suggestions on [topic]. Even if you think I'm good at this already, I'd appreciate your comments—please don't wait for me to ask."

2 Providing coaching—see, particularly, Chapters 5 and 6.

One minute (or longer) sessions of praise—where warranted. Most coachees do not listen when the typical manager provides positive feedback. Why? Because the coachee is waiting for the inevitable "but...," which normally follows and which heralds a series of suggestions for improved performance. By sometimes providing unmitigated praise, you will find your coachee becoming more attentive to your comments and more trusting of you.

Active illustration of how to accomplish the task at which the coachee is trying to build her/his skills. You can accomplish this by demonstration or by collaboration. For example, if you are helping the coachee to run meetings more effectively, you could demonstrate specific points by taking her/him along to one that you yourself are leading. Ask afterwards what she/he observed and what she/he might try differently next time (you could even ask for feedback on your own performance in running that meeting!).

Alternatively, you could collaborate—working with your coachee on a specific task. For example, if the coaching task is to analyze market research data with greater insight, you could work through the detailed data with your coachee so that she/he could see at first hand how insights can be generated.

You can obviously provide these active illustrations only if you yourself are relatively expert. If you lack the necessary expertise in the area in question, you should suggest a role model for the coachee to observe in action.

During these interactions, use the full repertoire of coaching tools which you now know about: the Ask/Tell spectrum (page 11), GROW (page 41), instant payoff coaching (page 64), pure feedback (page 32), motivation (page 81) and others.

3 **Concluding the coaching arrangement.** You will not want your coaching relationship to just fizzle out. Exactly how you con-

Figure 3

DEVELOPING A VISION

Encouragement, praise, and suggestion may not amount to anything without an engaging vision

clude it will depend on factors such as whether your coachee will, in any case, continue working with you or interacting with you socially. However, any conclusion should include at least three steps:

Reflection. Reflection is a critical aspect of how most people learn (see *Educating the Reflective Practitioner* by Schon, listed in Suggested Readings). Ensure that the coachee reviews and reflects upon what she/he has learned over the past few months.

Feedback to the coach. Your coachee can probably give you some useful summary feedback on your coaching approach even if she/he has been doing so previously. Make sure you ask for it, and reflect on the experience yourself.

Next steps. Decide whether this is "goodbye" or "au revoir"; or perhaps you have been coaching your partner at tennis, and it's time to swap roles.

Alex switched off the dictating machine, got up and stretched. He cast one more glance over the wine-dark sea and went indoors. He picked up the phone and called his secretary.

"I've been trying to get hold of you all afternoon," she said, "the Chairman would like a word with you."

Five minutes later he put the phone down, just as his wife was coming in from the pool. "Sarah, I've got some good news..."

The End

APPENDICES

These appendices aim to help you practice coaching in real life. Some provide a basis for you to evaluate yourself and to plan specific actions (1, 2, 4, 6, 8, 10); others provide tangible examples of how to apply a coaching technique (5, 7); the remainder can be photocopied and used with colleagues and team members (3, 8, 9), as the basis for more effective working relationships.

APPENDIX COACHING (SELF-) ASSESSMENT FORM

Answer the following questions for yourself and/or ask colleagues to complete a copy of this page based on their impressions of you.

HOW MANY TIMES IN THE LAST WEEK DID I...

_____   Provide unconditional praise

_____   Give constructive feedback

_____   Check a colleague's level of motivation

_____   Inspire a colleague

_____   Ask for feedback

_____   Consciously delegate a task

_____   Hold a really effective team meeting

_____   Provide upward feedback

_____   Check a team's morale

_____   Mentor a more junior person

_____   **TOTAL**

TOTALS

1 – 3 If you are not a recluse, you need to study and apply this book carefully.

4 – 6 You can significantly increase your effectiveness at work by applying just a few tips from this book.

7 – 8 You are nearly a master coach.

9 – 10 Give this book to someone who needs it.

PRIORITY AREAS FOR ME TO WORK ON

1

2

3

APPENDIX **Asking Versus Telling**

1. *Asking effective questions is one of the most powerful techniques of coaching. How often do you ask questions (even if you think you know the answer) in order to help build the understanding of an individual or team? Ask a few colleagues or friends for their perspectives on this, and summarize your current profile below:*

SITUATIONS WHERE I USE EFFECTIVE QUESTIONS

Appropriate

_____

_____

_____

_____

Inappropriate

_____

_____

_____

_____

SITUATIONS WHERE I SOMETIMES ASK, SOMETIMES TELL

Appropriate

_____

_____

_____

_____

Inappropriate

_____

_____

_____

_____

SITUATIONS WHERE I JUST TELL

Appropriate

_____

_____

_____

_____

Inappropriate

_____

_____

_____

_____

2. Identify the biggest risk you are willing to take in using an unfamiliar style from the ìask-tellî spectrum. Only by practicing will you be able to extend your repertoire:

Style to use:

_____

_____

Situation in which to apply it:

_____

_____

_____

Deadline for trying the style:

_____

3

APPENDIX GETTING FEEDBACK

To

_____

From

_____

I would like to get better at:

_____

As we work together over the next _____ weeks on

_____

I would appreciate any feedback or suggestions you could give me.

I think my current abilities in this area are as follows:

_____

_____

_____

Things I do well:

_____

_____

_____

Things I would like to practice:

_____

_____

_____

Things I would like you to show me how to do better:

_____

_____

_____

I would appreciate any feedback

        _____ immediately
        _____ at agreed weekly times
        _____ ad hoc

Is there any area in which you would like me to give you feedback?

_____

_____

_____

APPENDIX FEEDBACK PLAN

Three People to Whom I Could Give Feedback

1   Name

Topics to cover:

_____

_____

_____

Further information I need to gather:

_____

_____

_____

When I will provide feedback:

_____

2 Name

Topics to cover:

_____

_____

_____

Further information I need to gather:

_____

_____

_____

When I will provide feedback:

_____

3 Name

Topics to cover:

_____

_____

_____

Further information I need to gather:

_____

_____

_____

When I will provide feedback:

_____

5 APPENDIX EXAMPLES OF USEFUL QUESTIONS WHEN USING GROW

GOAL

What is it you would like to discuss?

What would you like to achieve?

What would you like from (to achieve in) this session?

What would need to happen for you to walk away feeling
that this time was well spent?

If I could grant you a wish for this session, what would it be?

What would you like to be different when you leave this session?

What would you like to happen that is not happening now,
or what would you like not to happen that is happening now?

What outcome would you like from this session/discussion/interaction?

Is that realistic?

Can we do that in the time we have available?

Will that be of real value to you?

REALITY

What is happening at the moment?

How do you know that this is accurate?

When does this happen?

How often does this happen? Be precise if possible.

What effect does this have?

How have you verified, or would you verify, that that is so?

What other factors are relevant?

Who else is relevant?

What is their perception of the situation?

What have you tried so far?

OPTIONS

What could you do to change the situation?

What alternatives are there to that approach?

Tell me what possibilities for action you see.
Do not worry about whether they are realistic at this stage.

What approach/actions have you seen used, or used yourself,
in similar circumstances?

Who might be able to help?

Would you like suggestions from me?

Which options do you like the most?

What are the benefits and pitfalls of these options?

Which options are of interest to you?

Rate from 1–10 your interest level in/the practicality of
each of these options.

Would you like to choose an option to act on?

WRAP-UP

What are the next steps?

Precisely when will you take them?

What might get in the way?

Do you need to log the steps in your diary?

What support do you need?

How and when will you enlist that support?

APPENDIX OVERCOMING COACHING BLOCKS

Even great coaches have some in-built reluctance to coach in certain situations. They are still able to be great coaches because they typically acknowledge their coaching blocks and find ways to work around them.

Because these blocks are usually embedded in the subconscious, the only way to accurately diagnose your own situation is to ask a particularly insightful friend (or psychologist) to characterize your avoidance mechanisms.

As an alternative—or in addition—try the following exercise. Although it does not identify your coaching blocks, it can help you to become even more courageous in addressing coaching situations that you find challenging.

1 *List 6 coaching situations in order of difficulty to you— for example: 1 = coaching a friend who asks you for help when you have time to give; 6 = giving "upward" feedback to a dictatorial boss.*

1 _____

2 _____

3 _____

4 _____

5 _____

6 _____

2   *Identify the most difficult situation with which you currently feel comfortable. Then move up one level on the difficulty scale and examine that situation.*

3   *List the reasons why the situation seems difficult or threatening. Then list five advantages to you of addressing it.*

Why threatening?

1 _____

2 _____

3 _____

Advantages of addressing situation?

1 _____

2 _____

3 _____

4   *Brainstorm ways to deal with the problem (use the Instant Payoff Coaching Technique–see Chapter 9).*

5   *Take a deep breath and give it a try.*

7

APPENDIX MORE DETAILS ON APPLYING THE SKILL/WILL MATRIX

Answer the following questions for yourself and/or ask colleagues to complete a copy of this page based on their impressions of you.

DIRECT (SKILL AND WILL ARE BOTH LOW)

First build the will:

> *Provide clear briefing.*

> *Identify motivations.*

> *Develop a vision of future performance.*

Then build the skill:

> *Structure tasks for "quick wins"*

> *Coach and train.*

Then sustain the will:

> *Provide frequent feedback.*

> *Praise and nurture.*

But supervise closely with tight control and clear rules/deadlines.

GUIDE (LOW SKILL, HIGH WILL)

Invest time early on:

> *Coach and train.*

> *Answer questions/explain.*

Create a risk-free environment to allow early mistakes/learning.

Relax control as progress is shown.

E X C I T E (high skill, low will)

Identify reason for low will—for example, task/management style/personal factors.

Motivate (see Chapter 12).

Monitor, feedback.

D E L E G A T E (skill and will are both high)

Provide freedom to do the job:

> *Set objective, not method.*

> *Praise, don't ignore.*

Encourage coachee to take responsibility:

> *Involve in decision-making.*

> *Use "You tell me what you think."*

Take appropriate risks:

> *Give more stretching tasks.*

> *Don't over-manage.*

8

APPENDIX MOTIVATION EXERCISES:
WHAT MOTIVATES YOU MOST/LEAST

*Have members of your team(s) complete copies of this
page and share their results.* (1 = HIGH 4 = LOW)

IMPORTANCE OF FACTOR	CURRENT SATISFACTION	**F A C T O R**
_____	_____	Manager showing concern for you as a person
_____	_____	Having some authority
_____	_____	Good personal relationships with manager
_____	_____	Manager's decisiveness
_____	_____	Examples provided by manager
_____	_____	Being involved in planning your own work
_____	_____	Recognition of your efforts
_____	_____	Delegation of work to you
_____	_____	Being promoted
_____	_____	Customer/client contact
_____	_____	Salary

IMPORTANCE OF FACTOR	CURRENT SATISFACTION	**F A C T O R**
_____	_____	Extent to which you get on with your peers
_____	_____	Praise
_____	_____	Attaining your own goals and meeting targets
_____	_____	Satisfaction with the job
_____	_____	Working conditions
_____	_____	Having responsibility for discrete areas of work
_____	_____	Working under pressure
_____	_____	A competitive environment
_____	_____	Your prospects of career development
_____	_____	Constructive feedback and coaching
_____	_____	Job security
_____	_____	The result of the completed work
_____	_____	Carrying out complex analysis
_____	_____	The organisation's structure and processes
_____	_____	Your personal job title

IMPORTANCE OF FACTOR	CURRENT SATISFACTION	**F A C T O R**
_____	_____	Extent of supervision
_____	_____	Social functions
_____	_____	Detailed guidance on how to complete work tasks
_____	_____	Working in a team
_____	_____	Being given clear objectives
_____	_____	Attending high-level meetings
_____	_____	Starting work early in the morning
_____	_____	Finishing work late in the evening
_____	_____	Other (specify)

APPENDIX

TEAM PERFORMANCE
APPRAISAL FORM

Ask members of your team to complete and discuss copies of this form. (1 = HIGH 4 = LOW)

CURRENT
RATING

GOAL
Indicator

_____

MEANINGFUL PURPOSE
All team members feel a common and meaningful sense of purpose behind the project and are clear on its value

Suggestions for Improvement

_____

_____

_____

_____

_____

_____

PERFORMANCE GOALS
The team is working towards achieving agreed goals in an effective manner

Suggestions for Improvement

_____

_____

_____

_____

_____

_____ **WORKING APPROACH**

All team members contribute to the 'real work' on the
project, and have a definite and positive role to play

Suggestions for Improvement

_____

_____

_____

_____

_____

All team members provide each other with satisfactory
real-time feedback

Suggestions for Improvement

_____

_____

_____

_____

_____

The team operates in a non-hierarchical manner
(i.e., team members feel that their contributions are
fully heard and appraised)

Suggestions for Improvement

_____

_____

_____

_____

_____

_____

COMPLEMENTARY SKILLS

The team has accessed the right mix of skills, directly
and indirectly

Suggestions for Improvement

_____

_____

_____

_____

_____

MUTUAL ACCOUNTABILITY

All team members feel that the achievement of the team
goals is recognised and regarded above individual contributions

Suggestions for Improvement

_____

_____

_____

_____

Team members provide mutual support and encouragement.
Each team member feels accountable for the team's success

Suggestions for Improvement

_____

_____

_____

_____

The team is providing opportunities and support to individuals in meeting their goals

Suggestions for Improvement

_____

_____

_____

_____

_____

OVERALL

The team has maintained a high level of morale

Suggestions for Improvement

_____

_____

_____

_____

_____

All team members have felt strongly motivated throughout this project

Suggestions for Improvement

_____

_____

_____

_____

_____

MENTORING

Mentoring is similar to coaching, but tends to endure for longer periods, be based on a deeper relationship, and address career issues rather than the building of task-specific skills. It plays a valuable role for individuals and organisations.

WHO HAS BEEN A MENTOR TO YOU?

Mentor's name:

_____

What did he/she do for you?

_____

_____

_____

_____

How did this help you?

_____

_____

_____

_____

Would other people appreciate similar help from you?

TO WHOM WILL YOU BE A MENTOR?

Mentee's name(s):

_____

What support will you provide them?

_____

_____

_____

_____

When will you start?

_____

How might this benefit you, as mentor?

_____

_____

_____

_____

SUGGESTED READING

COACHING

Blanchard, Kenneth H. & Spencer Johnson. *The One Minute Manager,* Morrow Publishing, New York, NY, 1982.

Blanchard, Ken & Don Shula. *Everyone's a Coach: Five Business Secrets for High-Performance Coaching,* Zondervan Publishing House, Grand Rapids, MI, 1995.

Bone, Diane. *The Business of Listening : A Practical Guide to Effective Listening,* Crisp Publications, Menlo Park, CA, 1995.

Gallwey, W. Timothy. *The Inner Game of Golf,* Random House, New York, NY, 1981.

———— *The Inner Game of Tennis,* Random House, New York, NY, 1974.

Gallwey, W. Timothy & Bob Kriegel. *Inner Skiing,* Random House, New York, NY, 1977.

Gilley, Jerry W. and Nathaniel W. Boughton. *Stop Managing, Start Coaching!: How Performance Coaching Can Enhance Commitment and Improve Productivity,* Irwin Professional Publishing, Chicago, IL, 1996.

Hendricks, William. *Coaching, Mentoring and Managing,* Career Press, Franklin Lakes, NJ, 1996.

Kinlaw, Dennis C. *Coaching for Commitment*, Pfeiffer & Company, San Francisco, CA, 1993.

Lowe, Phil. *Coaching and Counselling*, McGraw Hill, New York, NY, 1995.

Lucas, Robert. *Coaching Skills: A Guide for Supervisors*, Irwin Professional Publishing, Burr Ridge, IL, 1994.

MacLennan, Nigel. *Coaching and Mentoring*, Ashgate Publishing, Brookfield, VT, 1995.

Salisbury, Frank S. *Developing Managers As Coaches: A Trainer's Guide*, McGraw Hill, New York, NY, 1996.

Mentoring

Bell, Chip R. *Managers As Mentors: Building Partnerships for Learning*, Berrett-Koehler, San Francisco, CA, 1996.

Caldwell, Brian J., Earl M.A. Carter. *The Return of the Mentor: Strategies for Workplace Learning*, Falmer Publishing, London, 1993.

Clutterbuck, David. *Mentoring in Action: A Practical Guide for Managers*, Kogan Page Ltd., London, 1995.

Kram, Kathy E. *Mentoring at Work: Developmental Relationships in Organizational Life*, University Press of America, Lanham, MD, 1988.

Mink, Oscar G., Keith Q. Owen & Barbara P. Mink. *Developing High Performance People: The Art of Coaching*, Addison-Wesley Publishing Company, Reading, MA, 1993.

Murray, Margo. *Beyond the Myths and Magic of Mentoring: How to Facilitate an Effective Mentoring Program*, Jossey-Bass Mgmt. Series, San Francisco, CA, 1991.

Parsloe, Eric. *Coaching, Mentoring and Assessing: A Practical Guide to Developing Competence*, Nichols Publishing Company, New York, NY, 1992.

Shea, Gordon F. *Mentoring*, Crisp Publications, Menlo Park, CA, 1992.

Whitmore, John. *Coaching for Performance: A Practical Guide to Growing Your Own Skills*, Nicholas Brealey, London, 1994.

Psychology and Counseling

de Board, Robert. *Counselling Skills*, Wildwood House, London, 1987.

Garfield, Charles A. & Hal Zina Bennett. *Peak Performance: Mental Training Techniques of the World's Greatest Athletes*, J.P. Tarcher, Los Angeles, CA, 1984.

Gibb, Jack R. *Trust: A New View of Personal and Organizational Development*, Guild of Tutors Press, Los Angeles, CA, 1978.

Harris, Thomas A. *I'm OK, You're OK; A Practical Guide To Transactional Analysis*, Harper & Row, New York, NY, 1969.

Keirsey, David & Marilyn Bates. *Please Understand Me: Character and Temperament Types*, Prometheus Nemesis Book Company, Del Mar, CA, 1978.

Parkinson, Frank. *Listening and Helping in the Workplace: A Guide for Managers, Supervisors and Colleagues Who Need to Use Counselling Skills*, Souvenir Press Limited, London, 1996.

Whitmore, Diana. *Psychosynthesis: Counselling in Action*, Sage Publications Limited, London, 1991.

Learning

Argyris, Chris. *Overcoming Organizational Defenses: Facilitating Organizational Learning*, Allyn & Bacon, Boston, MA, 1990.

Brookfield, Stephen D. *Understanding and Facilitating Adult Learning*, Jossey-Bass Publishers, San Francisco, CA, 1986.

General

Bandler, Robert & John Grinder. *Frogs into Princes*, Real People Press, Moab, UT, 1979.

Bennis, Warren. *On Becoming a Leader*, Addison-Wesley Publishing Company, Reading, MA, 1989.

Covey, Stephen R. *The Seven Habits of Highly Effective People*, Simon & Schuster, New York, NY, 1989.

Hofstede, Geert. *Cultures and Organizations*, McGraw-Hill, New York, NY, 1991.

Katzenbach, Jon R. & Douglas K. Smith. *The Wisdom of Teams*, Harvard Business School Press, Boston, MA, 1993.

Schon, Donald A. *Educating the Reflexive Practitioner*, Jossey-Bass Publishers, San Francisco, CA, 1987.

Sturkie, Joan and Charles Hanson. *Leadership Skills for Peer Group Facilitators*, Resource Publications, San Jose, CA, 1992.

ACKNOWLEDGMENTS

This book is the product of several teams, and I would like to thank all of my teammates. First, I thank my many colleagues from across McKinsey & Company who contributed to the original guide to our coaching program, on which this book is based. In particular, I thank Sandra Charalambous, Humphrey Cobbold, Kate Grussing, Andrew Glover, Judith Hazlewood, Julian Seaward, Frazer Smith, Kathryn Thomas, and Jim Wendler for their help.

Norman Sanson, until recently McKinsey's U.K. Managing Director, deserves special acknowledgment. He not only had the vision to launch our initial coaching program, but also contributed through strong personal example. I am also indebted to my other partners around the globe for their support, particularly Ian Davis who currently leads our U.K. practice.

Ben Cannon also had a major impact on this book by personally coaching me, and by contributing several chapters based on his years of expertise in the field. Peter Bamford, Managing Director (retail) of W.H. Smith, kindly suggested improvements based on his experience as manager, coach, and retailer of books.

I should also like to thank the McKinsey team responsible for the production of this book: Partha Bose (Director of Communications,

Europe) provided both incisive comment and strong personal encourage-ment. Robert Whiting (Publications Editor) and Deborah Thomas (Edi-tor) added continuity to the story and removed anachronism and zeugma. Carole Gardner, Alison Mills and Steph Saul creatively enhanced the book's format.

On the publishing side, I would like to thank two teams: Martin Liu, Lucinda McNeile, and Juliet Van Oss at HarperCollins, and Cindy Ku-magawa, Lorraine Spurge, and Kenin Spivak at Knowledge Exchange. They each made a major contribution to either the U.K. edition or the U.S. version of the book. In one way or another they each taught me how important it is for an author to be a good coachee!

Finally I thank HIGGINS, whose cartoons still make me laugh on the twentieth rereading, for being a creative guru, pictorial master, and out-standing collaborator.

INDEX

Knowledge Exchange
Business Solutions System

As part of Knowledge Exchange's commitment to producing and disseminating the most useful and beneficial business knowledge available, we are proud to launch our new Business Solutions System. In order to provide a full range of products, this System will include practical, comprehensive, full-color, illustrated encyclopedias, dictionaries, and industry and trade books that cover all aspects of eight critical business disciplines.

Included in the Business Solutions System are backlist titles under the categories of Reference Essentials, Management Consultant, Entrepreneurial Advisor, and Industry Expert.

KEX was founded in 1989 by President and CEO Lorraine Spurge. Formerly a senior vice president at Drexel Burnham Lambert (1983–1989), she raised more than $200 billion for companies including MCI Communications, Turner Broadcasting, Viacom, Barnes & Nobles, Mattel, and Tele-Communications, Inc.

KEX Chairman of the Board, Kenin M. Spivak, is also Cofounder, President, and Co–CEO of Archon Communications, Inc. He has served as President of the Island World Group; Executive Vice President and COO of MGM/UA Communications Co.; and Vice President of Merrill Lynch Investment Banking. He is also an attorney and a film producer.

For more information about the company or its products, visit the KEX Web site at http://www.kex.com or write to: Knowledge Exchange LLC, Publicity Dept., 1299 Ocean Ave. Suite 250, Santa Monica, CA 90401.

REFERENCE ESSENTIALS SERIES

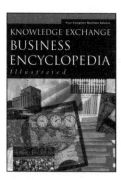

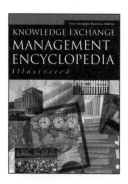

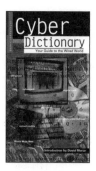

Knowledge Exchange Business Encyclopedia

Your Complete Business Advisor

Lorraine Spurge, Editor in Chief

ISBN: 1-888232-05-6
750 pages 7 1/2 x 10 1/2
Business/Reference
$45.00 hardcover
(In Canada: $54.00)
Rights: World

The ultimate business tool and the ultimate business gift, this illustrated reference book provides a wealth of information and advice on eight critical disciplines: accounting, economics, finance, marketing, management, operations, strategy, and technology.

Knowledge Exchange Management Encyclopedia

Your Complete Business Advisor

Lorraine Spurge, Editor in Chief

ISBN: 1-888232-32-3
448 pages 7 1/2 x 10 1/2
Business/Reference
$28.00 hardcover
(In Canada: $34.95)
Rights: World

Volume two of the Business Encyclopedia series, this book is an essential management tool providing in-depth information on hundreds of key management terms, techniques, and practices—and practical advice on how to apply them to your business.

CyberDictionary

Your Guide to the Wired World

Edited and Introduced by David Morse

ISBN: 1-888232-04-8
336 pages 5 1/4 x 9 1/4
Reference/Computer
$17.95 softcover
(In Canada: $21.95)
Rights: World

In clear, concise language, *CyberDictionary* makes sense of the wide-open frontier of cyberspace with information useful to the novice and the cyber-pro alike.

MANAGEMENT CONSULTANT SERIES

The Accelerated Transition®

Fast Forward Through Corporate Change

Mark L. Feldman, Ph.D. and Michael F. Spratt, Ph.D.

ISBN: 1-888232-28-5
225 pages 6 1/4 x 9 1/4
Business/Management
$22.95 hardcover
(In Canada: $28.95)
Rights: World

After the deal is done, many mergers fail. Why? Because the companies are poor matches and managers are unable to integrate disparate corpo-

rate cultures, thus causing management to be unsuccessful at achieving the goals that motivated the merger in the first place. The result? Company after company plunges into organizational upheaval and becomes unable to realize potential rewards.

Authored by America's top consultants on implementing corporate mergers, Mark L. Feldman, Ph.D., and Michael F. Spratt, Ph.D., *The Accelerated Transition®* provides critical lessons on how to turn major reorganizations into truly productive makeovers. Most important are intensive planning and speedy execution (once a merger closes, a transition should take only about 100 days).

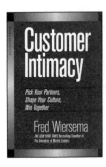

Customer Intimacy

Pick Your Partners, Shape Your
Culture, Win Together

Fred Wiersema

ISBN: 1-888232-00-5
240 pages 6 1/4 x 9 1/4
Business/Marketing
$22.95 hardcover
(In Canada: $27.95)
Rights: World
Audiobook
ISBN: 1-888232-01-3
$14.00 (In Canada: $17.00)
90 minutes/Read by the author

One in three market-leading companies attains prominence today by making the most of what author Fred
Wiersema calls "customer intimacy."
This engaging book reveals why the
most successful businesses are those
that build close win-win relationships
with their customers.

Richly illustrated with examples of
some of the best-known and most successful customer-intimate businesses,
Customer Intimacy is for companies
wondering what to do next after having exhausted the potential of quality
thinking, lean management, and business reengineering.

Fad-Free Management

The Six Principles That Drive
Successful Companies and Their
Leaders

Richard Hamermesh

ISBN: 1-888232-20-X
208 pages 6 1/4 x 9 1/4
Business/Management
$24.95 hardcover
(In Canada: $29.95)
Rights: World

The business place has become satu-
rated with quick fixes that promise
faster, better products and happier,
more loyal employees. Unfortunately,
however, these fads often waste time
and energy. In this new book, Richard
Hamermesh argues against this trend
and stresses the necessity of getting
back to basics.

Readers of **Fad-Free Management**
will reap the benefits of the knowledge
Hamermesh gained as a professor at
the world-renowned Harvard Business
School.

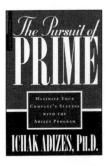

The Pursuit of Prime

Maximize Your Company's
Success with the Adizes Program

Ichak Adizes, Ph.D.

ISBN: 1-888232-22-6
304 pages 6 1/4 x 9 1/4
Business/Management
$24.95 hardcover
(In Canada: $29.95)
Rights: World

Companies, like people, follow definite
growth stages—infancy, childhood,
adolescence, and *prime*. It is in this last
stage of development that both
humans and companies are at their
best. In **The Pursuit of Prime,** Ichak
Adizes, Ph.D., provides a step-by-step
guide for helping businesses reach this
pinnacle of corporate life.

The Pursuit of Prime provides case
studies of successful companies such
as Bank of America and the Body Shop
and enumerates the bad habits,
philosophies, and myths that prevent
companies from being attuned to their
life cycles and thereby prosperous.

The Tao of Coaching

Boost Your Effectiveness by
Inspiring Those Around You

Max Landsberg

ISBN: 1-888232-34-X
200 pages 6 1/4 x 9 1/4
Business/Management
$22.95 hardcover
Rights: U.S.

Get the most out of your human capital—your employees—by transforming
them into all-star managers and team
players. Ideally, managers should be
coaches who enhance the performance and learning abilities of others.
They must provide feedback, motivation, and a master game plan.

In **The Tao of Coaching** Max Landsberg shares his belief that managers
must possess a broad repertoire of
management styles. The coaching skills
managers can acquire from reading
this book will allow them to diagnose
different employee styles and use
appropriate means to bring out the
best in all individuals they work with.

ENTREPRENEURIAL ADVISOR SERIES

Failure Is Not an Option

How MCI Invented Competition in Telecommunications

Lorraine Spurge

ISBN: 1-888232-08-0
272 pages 6 1/4 x 9 1/4
Business/Finance
$22.95 hardcover
(In Canada: $27.95)
Rights: World

Educational and entertaining, **Failure Is Not an Option** profiles MCI's stirring history from its meager beginnings to its present success, offering an enlightening view of the financial, management, and marketing issues the company faced. Readers will experience the tension and suspense as MCI fights for survival, takes on AT&T (then the mightiest corporation in the world), shakes up federal regulatory agencies, races to raise desperately needed capital, and ultimately alters forever the American business landscape.

Failure Is Not an Option features a two-color layout sprinkled with charts, graphs, photos, and time lines illustrating the history of MCI and the telecommunications industry in general.

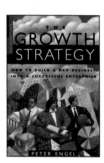

The Growth Strategy

How to Build a New Business Into a Successful Enterprise

Peter Engel

ISBN: 1-888232-30-7
240 pages 6 1/4 x 9 /1/4
Business/Entrepreneur
$22.95 hardcover
(In Canada: $28.95)
Rights: World

The Growth Strategy is a step-by-step guide on how entrepreneurs can help their companies make the transition from the start-up phase to a professionally managed business.

This book will show entrepreneurs in the midst of this transition how to:

- Develop a strong business from an entrepreneurial venture
- Create a valuable business that can be sold at a profit or taken public
- Grow beyond niche markets

The Growth Strategy profiles dozens of well-known companies such as Procter & Gamble, Federal Express, and Compaq, and demonstrates how they were transformed into successes through the power of aggressive growth.

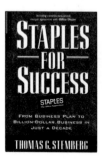

Staples for Success

From Business Plan to Billion-Dollar Business in Just a Decade

Thomas G. Stemberg

ISBN: 1-888232-24-2
192 pages 6 1/4 x 9 1/4
Business
$22.95 hardcover
(In Canada: $27.95)
Rights: World

Audiobook
ISBN: 1-888232-25-0
$12.00 (In Canada: $15.00)
60 minutes/Read by Campbell Scott

This engaging story details Staples' birth and subsequent transformation into office-superstore giant. Stemberg's hard work and commitment to excellence turned a radically simple idea into the $11 billion office-superstore industry we know today. The Staples story stands as a guide to forward thinking and successful management from genesis to innovation to large-scale, almost limitless growth.

Staples for Success is a must-read for every entrepreneur and anyone who believes in a great idea.

The World On Time

The 11 Management Principles That Made FedEx an Overnight Sensation

James C. Wetherbe

ISBN: 1-888232-06-4
200 pages 6 1/4 x 9 1/4
Business/Management
$22.95 hardcover
(In Canada: $27.95)
Rights: World

Audiobook
ISBN: 1-888232-07-2
$12.00 (In Canada: $15.00)
90 minutes/Read by the author

The World On Time is the inspirational story of how Federal Express became a leader in the overnight-delivery industry.

James C. Wetherbe, a preeminent business consultant and academic, provides a richly detailed, intimate portrait of Federal Express. Readers will learn how eleven innovative management strategies employed by Federal Express have set the standard for the way companies manage time and information, plan logistics, and serve customers.

Changing Health Care

Creating Tomorrow's Winning Health Enterprise Today

Ken Jennings, Ph.D., Kurt Miller, and Sharyn Materna of Andersen Consulting

ISBN: 1-888232-18-8
336 pages   6 1/4 x 9 1/4
Business/Health Care
$24.95 hardcover
(In Canada: $29.95)
Rights: World

One of the major health care tasks is to deliver more value to consumers through better and expanded products and services. *Changing Health Care* outlines the strategies that all health care organizations must adopt

if they want to regain their competitive edge.

The authors propose eight winning strategies designed to keep health care providers on the cutting edge— Keep Ahead of Consumers; Keep the Promise; Cut to the Moment of Value; Mind the Cycle of Life; Capitalize on Knowledge; Ride the Technology Wave; Give Your Best, Virtualize the Rest; and Mine the Riches of Outcomes.

Changing Health Care is an incisive wake-up call to the health care industry. It challenges health care providers to join the reengineering revolution reshaping American business—or face ruin.

Prescription for the Future

How the Technology Revolution Is Changing the Pulse of Global Health Care

Gwendolyn B. Moore, David A. Rey, and John D. Rollins of Andersen Consulting

ISBN: 1-888232-10-2
200 pages   6 1/4 x 9 1/4
Business/Health Care
$24.95 hardcover
(In Canada: $29.95)
Rights: World

Audiobook
ISBN: 1-888232-11-0
$12.00 (In Canada: $15.00)
60 minutes/Read by the authors

Authored by leading experts from the world's largest consulting firm, *Prescription for the Future* profiles an industry undergoing transformation and offers insights into the challenges facing the health care industry as it employs new technologies. This book directly addresses the concerns of managers and professionals in the health care industry regarding rapidly advancing information technology, which creates both new freedoms and new problems.

Like the *Knowledge Exchange Business Encyclopedia,* the next five volumes in the in-depth Reference Essentials series—*Management, Marketing, Corporate Finance, Personal Finance & Investment,* and *Entrepreneurism*—are easy-to-use, comprehensive reference books. Each specialized encyclopedia presents tools and techniques unique to its discipline and is illustrated with lustrous, full-color graphics.

▲ Access thousands of essential business terms and in-depth definitions

▲ Track the evolution of global industries

▲ Discover innovative businesspeople—past and present

▲ Learn from hundreds of mini case studies, tips, and insights from renowned experts

▲ Utilize numerous formulas and custom-designed charts and graphs

▲ Get free online access to up-to-date information

Your Complete Business Advisor

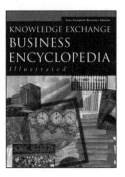

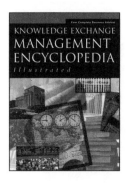

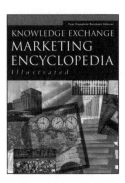

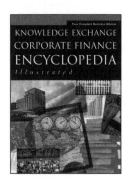

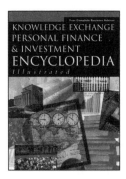

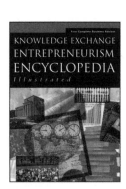

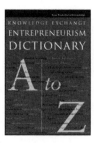

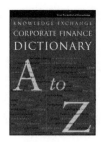

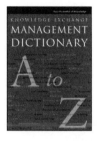

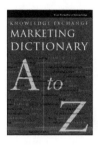

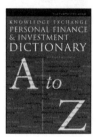

Another facet of the Reference Essentials Series is the *Knowledge Exchange Dictionaries*. These easy-to-carry dictionaries are designed to provide concise and easily accessible definitions to hundreds of terms in specialized topics including

▲ *Entrepreneurism*

▲ *Corporate Finance*

▲ *Management*

▲ *Marketing*

▲ *Personal Finance and Investment*

Each user-friendly, illustrated dictionary expands on hundreds of basic definitions with numerous examples, tips, traps, and other special elements adapted from the *Business Encyclopedia* series.

Your Pocketful of Knowledge

A Brief History of Business

A short, lavishly illustrated history of business is contained in this companion to *A Chronology of Business* poster. This book focuses on the interchange of three major areas—technology, business organization, and banking—and shows how breakthroughs in these areas helped determine the various directions that business took. Additionally, it outlines how the nature of these changes has accelerated during the past two centuries. Written by Robert Sobel. Editor in Chief: Lorraine Spurge.

(Coming to bookstores in 1997)

A Chronology of Business Poster

Limited Edition!

Available only from Knowledge Exchange, the full-color, exquisitely detailed *A Chronology of Business* poster (22"x 40") is based on the time line featured in the *Knowledge Exchange Business Encyclopedia*, which traces the history of business from its roots in 3000 B.C. to the present.

$25

I'd like to purchase the following products:

Number of copies

_____ **Knowledge Exchange Business Encyclopedia**

_____ **Knowledge Exchange Management Encyclopedia**

_____ **Changing Health Care**

_____ **Customer Intimacy**
_____ Also available as an audiobook

_____ **CyberDictionary**

_____ **Fad-Free Management**

_____ **The Growth Strategy**

_____ **Prescription for the Future**
_____ Also available as an audiobook

_____ **Staples for Success**
_____ Also available as an audiobook

_____ **The Pursuit of Prime**

_____ **The Tao of Coaching**

_____ **The World On Time**
_____ Also available as an audiobook

_____ **A Chronology of Business Poster**

_____ **Knowledge Exchange Business Encyclopedia Canvas Tote Bag**
(See last page.)

Free Business • Reference • Finance Tote with Purchase of Three Books!*

Name_____ E-mail_____

Company_____ Title_____

Address_____

City/State/Zip_____

Telephone_____ Fax_____

Form of Payment:

❏ Check (payable to **Knowledge Exchange,** LLC)   ❏ Credit card

Card #_____Exp. Date _____Card Type_____

Cardholder's Signature: _____

Tell us more about yourself:

Occupation	Where do you buy business books?	How many business books do you buy a year?	Age Group
❏ Management	❏ Bookstore	❏ 0–3	❏ 18–24
❏ Marketing	❏ Mail Order	❏ 4–10	❏ 25–34
❏ Finance	❏ Warehouse Store	❏ 11–15	❏ 35–49
❏ Administrative	❏ Other	❏ 16 or more	❏ 50–over
❏ Sales			
❏ Other			

Knowledge Exchange products are available wherever books are sold.
To order by fax, photocopy this page and fax to 714.261.6137
or call toll-free to order with your credit card.

Telephone 1-888-394-5996 or Fax 1-714-261-6137

*Offer expires December 31, 1998 or while supplies last.
Shipping and handling is $4.95 for the first book, $1 for each additional book, $2 additional for each *Business Encyclopedia.*
Shipping is via Priority Mail. California residents please add 8.25% sales tax.

All About Knowledge Exchange Business Collectibles

Knowledge Exchange Business Encyclopedia Canvas Tote Bag

Vibrantly colored, heavy-duty, natural canvas, oversized tote bag (14"h x 16"w x 9"d) displaying the Knowledge Exchange logo, which is surrounded by a sampling of terms and references cited in the *Knowledge Exchange Business Encyclopedia.*

$50